THE SPIRIT OF
SHINTO

Dedicated to my mother,
a Christian woman who taught me to be
inquisitive and to never stop learning.
On her trips to Japan, we have visited numerous
Shintoist shrines together. Each time we pass
through a *torii* gate, she starts to ask me
questions that I can't always answer.
In this book I try to answer her questions, which
might resonate with other restless minds
interested in Japanese culture.

THE SPIRIT OF SHINTO

SHINTO

Finding Nature *and* Harmony *on* Japan's Sacred Path

Héctor García

Translated by
Russell Andrew Calvert

TUTTLE Publishing

Tokyo | Rutland, Vermont | Singapore

Contents

Japan's First Religion

Shinto originated in Japan and is considered to be the indigenous Japanese religion.

Along with Buddhism, it is one of the most widespread religious traditions in Japan. Buddhism and its philosophy have been written about at great length in the West, to the point where the practice of meditation has become a global phenomenon. On the other hand, Shinto is still wrapped in a halo of mystery.

This book's mission is to unravel the keys to Shinto in order to help us better understand the Japanese psyche, to comprehend their culture, literature, cinema and videogames in more depth, and to get greater enjoyment from our trips to the land of the rising sun. We shall also discover lessons and ideas that we can apply to improve our lives.

The word Shinto is written 神道 *shintō,* and is made up of two characters, which can be broken down like this:

神

There are several ways to pronounce it, including "*shin*" and "*kami.*"

It may be translated as: spirit, supernatural entity or god.

道

There are several ways to pronounce it, including "*to,*" "*michi,*" and "*dō.*"

It may be translated as: path, or the way or method of attaining something.

Thus, Shinto is "The way of the gods." But I prefer to say: "The way of the *kami,*" since, as we shall see in the following chapters, the concept of *kami* is quite different from the idea of God that we tend to have in the West.

I shall use the word *kami* (untranslated) to help our minds free themselves from preconceived ideas. Sometimes, to avoid tautologies, I shall also use spirit, god, deity, goddess, etc. but always referring to the same Japanese concept. In the Japanese language, no distinction is made between the plural and singular forms; I shall write *kami* without the letter "s" at the end for both cases.

Worship of and respect for the *kami* are the cornerstones of Shinto.

The *kami* live inside trees, rocks, mountains, plants, rivers and the sea; as a result, Shinto is classified as a religion of nature. It is also an animistic religion because it believes many of the phenomena that occur in the world may be explained by the divine actions of the *kami*.

Finally, Shinto is a polytheistic religion. The popular saying "eight million *kami*" (*Yaoyorozu no kami*) puts a figure on it but this number is less important than the idea it puts across to us that there is an unimaginable, perhaps infinite, number of *kami*.

After twenty years of living in Japan, I owe a lot to this place and its people. Between my first visit to a Shintoist shrine—on which I understood almost nothing but was completely spellbound by the aura of the place—and now, I have changed and am no longer the same person. I have visited thousands of Shintoist shrines, I married an Okinawan woman in a Shintoist shrine and each year at the start of January I go with my wife to celebrate *hatsumode* in the Meiji Jingū shrine.

The Japanese people and Shinto have both transformed me as a person.

I would go so far as to say Shinto is almost a synonym for Japan. Knowing Japanese culture helps us to comprehend Shinto, and vice versa; studying Shinto will open the doors to us to an understanding of Japanese culture.

Dr. Sokyo Ono, a former professor at Kokugakuin University, for whom I had the honor to write the foreword for the fiftieth anniversary of his book *Shinto—The Kami Way* (Tuttle Publishing), spent his whole life studying Shinto and said: "It is impossible to make explicit and clear that which fundamentally by its very nature is vague." He is referring to both Shinto and this country's culture. Hence, this book is merely a humble attempt to shed some light on the mentality on which this millenary society was built.

*"The first charm of Japan is intangible
and volatile as perfume."*

– Lafcadio Hearn,
Glimpses of Unfamiliar Japan, First Series (English Edition)

Fundamental Aspects of Shinto

Throughout this book, we shall take a closer look at each one of the fundamental aspects of Shinto, as summed up in the following table.

NATURE	Nature is inherent to almost all of the elements of Shinto. The *kami* are part of nature, as are humans; shrines and forests are in harmony and mountains are sacred.
ANIMISM	Spirits (*kami*) can inhabit any natural object or element. The *kami* may be deemed to be the energy that gives life and moves the universe. They live with us in this material world and can also be in other ethereal planes.
PURIFICATION	Many of the Shintoist rituals are centered on purification, or at least are partly devoted to it. Immoral actions "dirty" us or may anger the *kami*. Visiting shrines and participating in rituals purifies us.

PROTECTION	Belief in elements, which protect us against malevolent forces, illnesses, accidents, bad luck, etc.
WORSHIP OF ANCESTORS	Emphasis on worship of and respect for our ancestors. For centuries Japan was influenced by the cult of ancestors that is integral to Chinese Confucianism.
NO FOUNDER, DOCTRINES OR COMMAND-MENTS	Shinto has no founder, neither male nor female. Nor is there any scripture establishing doctrines, commandments, or precepts. There are though moral lessons in the shape of fables, tales and mythology. Much of the mythology is conserved in written form in the *Nihon Shoki* (日本書紀, *The Chronicles of Japan*) and the *Kojiki* (古事記, *Records of Ancient Matters*), both compiled at the beginning of the thirteenth century CE.
IDENTITY AND CONVERSION	People tend not to identify with the Shintoist tradition. That is to say, hardly anyone says, "I'm a Shintoist." Even if you ask the monks (*kannushi* or *miko*) working in or running shrines it is very common for them not to self-identify with the Shintoist label. For example, a *kannushi* or a *miko* can be Buddhist or Christian and still work in a Shintoist shrine. Nor is there a process of conversion to or union with Shinto, unlike in other religions.

EMPHASIS ON PUTTING THE PRACTICE OF RITUALS AHEAD OF BELIEFS	Shinto contains a plethora of beliefs that have evolved over thousands of years. As well as those related to nature, many of them were imported from Buddhism, Taoism, Confucianism and *onmyōdō*. Although beliefs are important, the emphasis in Shinto is on the practice of rituals, which go from something as simple as visiting a shrine to more complex celebrations such as the *matsuri* (festivals devoted to the *kami*).

"Shinto is essentially a religion of gratitude and love."

– W.G. Aston[1]

---

[1] Wikipedia contributors, "William George Aston," Wikipedia, The Free Encyclopedia, https://en.wikipedia.org/w/index.php?title=William_George_Aston&oldid=1241276253

Reflection on Spirituality, Eastern and Western Thinking

"If you know the way broadly, you will see it in everything."
— Miyamoto Musashi

I was raised in a culture (Spain, Europe) and at a time (1980s –1990s) in which a certain tension prevailed between the domains of reason and beliefs. As a child I used to go to church with my grandmother. She taught my brother and I to say the Lord's Prayer and the Ten Commandments. But instead of reading the Bible, I read Carl Sagan books, Isaac Asimov novels and Japanese manga. Later, I began to study for a degree in computer engineering and after a brief spell at CERN, one of the largest scientific laboratories in Europe, I moved to Japan.

Until I reached twenty years of age, my only understanding of what a religion or a belief system involved was based on Abrahamic traditions. That is to say, there is only one Almighty God, who as it turns out doesn't live here with us on planet Earth, but in another place. This God created human beings in his own image and likeness (in Latin: *imago dei*), He looks after us and also watches over all of us; we must not sin if we desire salvation.

On arriving here in Tokyo, one of the first culture shocks I felt was when noticing how there was a blurring of lines in the behavior of both individuals and society in general when it came to beliefs, superstitions, science and reason—they all merged into a hard to separate amalgamation. Over time, after many trips around Asia, I learned that the coexistence of beliefs and religions with science and reason is commonplace in this continent.

In anthropological studies the two mentalities are compared using the terms ("Western thinking" vs "Eastern thinking"). Of course, this dichotomy goes beyond religions and science and we can sometimes fall into generalizations and qualify something as an Eastern or Western way of thinking or not, but I believe it is a good tool for helping us to understand how the people of each culture see and feel the world.

One of the fundamental principles of "Eastern thinking" is that humans can choose from many paths in search of the truth, but none of them are universally valid for all of us.

No guru is going to take you by the hand and give you the answers to your questions about life. Each one of us must plot our own path. You are the one who has to climb to the summit of your own mountain. The hill is a metaphor for the life that only you can discover.

This mountain-climbing analogy is inspired by Taoist tradition.

Taoism influenced Buddhism, Confucianism, Hinduism and also Shinto. Its fundamental principle is that in any learning or experience in our lives, 道 (pronounced *dō* in Japanese, *dao* in Chinese) is the path or guide to follow.

This character exists in many Japanese words related to the arts: *judō* 柔道 (martial art, the literal translation is: the way of flexibility), *shodō* 書道 (art of calligraphy, the literal translation is: the way of writing), *sadō* 茶道 (art of the tea ceremony, the literal translation is: "the way of tea"), *kendō* 剣道 (martial art, the literal translation is: "the way of the sword"), *kyūdō* 弓道 (archery, the literal translation is: "the way of the bow").

As we saw in the previous section, the word *shintō* 神道 (Shinto) also contains the character *dō* 道 and is therefore "the way of the *kami*."

Miyamoto Musashi was a warrior and philosopher who lived through the transition to the Edo Period (late sixteenth and early seventeenth centuries), a period in which a melting pot of religions (Buddhism, Shinto, Taoism, etc.) coexisted and influenced one another. Although he was not a follower of any religion in particular, Miyamoto Musashi was inspired by and absorbed concepts from Buddhism, Confucianism, Shinto and Taoism, incorporating them into his life as an artist and warrior.

At the age of sixty, a week before his death (in early June 1645), he wrote twenty-one precepts on a parchment entitled *Dokkōdō* with his conclusions, or life lessons. The first of them is: *Yoyo no michi o somuku koto* 世々の道をそむく事, which literally translates as: "Do not disobey the path 道 marked out by previous generations." Other common translations of this precept are: "We must not leave the path marked out by the universe" or "Accept everything just the way it is."[2]

There is an evident emphasis on "the generations"—Miyamoto Musashi was clearly influenced here by the Confucianism of Ancient China, a philosophy that afforded great importance to the generational legacy.

The way in which the first precept is written implies that we must "accept" things, events and the nature of the universe just as they are. "Acceptance" is one of the fundamental principles of Buddhist tradition; it defends the idea that humans will only be released from suffering when we learn to accept reality without putting up resistance. Suffering increases when we swim against the tide, opposing nature, but we can train our mind and spirit to "accept."

And finally, it uses the Chinese character 道 (in this case pronounced "*michi*") with the metaphorical meaning of following our path in life—a clear and direct influence of Taoism.

The mixture of concepts and ideas from multiple philosophies and religions just seen in the first phrase of Miyamoto Musashi's *Dokkōdō* above is a constant in the history of Japan. In Chapter 7 we shall look in more depth at syncretism and the most important influential movements from other cultures, with particular reference to the arrival of Buddhism in the sixth century CE.

Many times I have asked Japanese people if they believe in the *kami*, in a god or gods, and I have almost never received a

---

[2] First precept from Miyamoto Musashi's *Dokkodo*. Wikipedia contributors, "Dokkōdō," *Wikipedia, The Free Encyclopedia*, https://en.wikipedia.org/w/index.php?title=Dokk%C5%8Dd%C5%8D&oldid=1241487337

straight answer. Most of them answer indirectly: "I don't know about a god but I believe there are many spirits," "Maybe there are *kami,* but there is no way of knowing," "When I go to a shrine I ask the *kami* to protect me," "At my parents' house we have an altar where we place incense for our ancestors," "I don't believe there are literally fairies in the woods but I usually go to my neighborhood temple with my wife," "I always have an *omamori* hanging in the car just in case—I believe it helps me avoid traffic accidents."

A few years ago, I was visiting a shrine in a little village in Yamanashi. It was a secluded out of the way place. I was taking photos of the sunset, capturing the shrine's roof and the silhouette of Mount Fuji on the horizon. It was silent except for the occasional bird tweeting.

Suddenly, two children turned up, chattering away in high spirits, almost shouting. Their conversation seemed so innocent to me, and at the same time so full of wisdom, that on returning to the *ryokan* where I was staying I wrote it down in my diary.

"I don't believe in anything," said one of them.

"There are lots of *kami* in this shrine," said the other.

"Seriously? I can't see them."

"Idiot! It's not about seeing them but feeling them."

"Well, I don't feel anything either."

"Idiot! It doesn't matter. What's important is to follow the ritual and show respect."

"Okay."

"You have to bow twice, clap your hands twice and then close your eyes."

The two children positioned themselves opposite the *haiden* and after they had clapped twice, we were once more enveloped by silence, with Mount Fuji watching over all of us from afar.

When they opened their eyes, they didn't say anything. They left in silence and only when they passed through the gate did I hear them talking in the distance.

The story of the two boys is an ideal example to help us reflect on the importance of spirituality, beyond believing in gods or supernatural entities. In the modern world, we are sold the idea that in order to be successful, we have to achieve lots of objectives one after the other, just as though we were collecting coins, stamps or virtual prizes in a video game.

Rituals are more important than objectives.

The mere act of praying or carrying out a ritual helps us more than achieving an objective does.

More and more scientific studies are analyzing the benefits of praying and meditating. What almost all the world's spiritual traditions have in common is something as simple as taking a few instants to relax, reflect and be with yourself.

The effectiveness of these practices is undeniable. The practice of meditation (which originated in Buddhism) is one of the most effective methods for treating problems of stress, anxiety and depression. You could say that Siddhartha Gautama was the first psychologist in history. Over the last few decades, Jon Kabat-Zinn has developed *mindfulness* drawing from the results of studies carried out on different kinds of meditation. Mindfulness is practiced by millions of people all around the world.

The field of neurotheology, or the neuroscience of religion, aims to explain religious practices and behaviors from the perspective of neuroscience. It looks for correlations between the practice of rituals (dances, prayers, meditation, etc.) and changes in our physiology (hormonal, neuronal, cardiac coherence, etc.).

In the 2000s, researchers at the University of Wisconsin subjected individuals to a study using fMRI. The person who produced the most gamma waves (associated with calmness and well-being) turned out to be Mattieu Ricard, a Buddhist monk who had been meditating for decades. Mattieu Ricard was named by the media as "the happiest man in the world."

At that time, I had just arrived in Japan and started to read books about Buddhism, Hinduism, and Eastern thinking, among them *The Monk and the Philosopher: A Father and Son Discuss the Meaning of Life*. In this book Mattieu Ricard has a dialogue with his father Jean-François Revel (a famous French philosopher) about why Mattieu gave up his promising scientific career in

France to emigrate to the mountains of Tibet to study Buddhism. They also converse about the nature of human consciousness, about what the role of science and religions is in the modern world, about why suffering, hate and wars exist... This and other books, like *Confession of a Buddhist Atheist* by Stephen Batchelor, gradually changed my attitude toward religious traditions and my understanding of them; I came to have greater appreciation for the value they add to human experience and the role they play as a social lubricant in cultures and societies.

Of course, the pathological use of religions, philosophies, beliefs and/or traditions, radicalizing them (taking ideas out of context or reinterpreting them) for political purposes, to manipulate and to exert power over groups of people is something that also occurs and we have seen it cause pain on many occasions in history. There was also a period in which Shinto was used for ideological purposes and directly controlled by the government in order to manipulate society's opinion. This Shinto is known in the history books as State Shintō (国家神道 *Kokka shintō*) and its power spread from the Meiji Period (second half of the nineteenth century) until the year 1945. The Allies ordered the government to issue a decree (the Shintō Directive) which established a separation of the state and religions and prohibited the use of Shinto for ideological purposes.

Leaving aside this period of State Shintō, in this book we shall focus on learning about the origins of Shinto, studying *ko-shintō* (古神道: Old Shinto) and current-day Shinto, known as *jinja-shintō* (神社神道: Shrine Shinto).

During the two decades I have lived in Japan, I have visited hundreds, if not thousands, of Shintoist shrines and Buddhist temples, I have read a plethora of books on Eastern philosophy, and I have traveled and conversed with people from many parts of Asia. Gradually, my world vision has become increasingly aligned with "Eastern thinking."

Another important concept I have taken on board during my life here is (ontological) dualism. According to Western thinking, there is the deeply rooted idea of a separation between our "mind-spirit" (immaterial world) and "body-rest of the universe" (material world). This dichotomy has permeated our way of thinking ever since Plato, with his *Phaedo*, or *On the Soul* dialogue, introduced the idea that the world in which we live is an imperfect reflection of a universe of forms. Even Aristotle, who differed on many points of philosophy, agreed with Plato's vision as far as the migration of souls was concerned. The two of them laid the foundations of what in the future would become one of the bases of the Abrahamic religions' worldview.

Centuries later Descartes said, "*Cogito, ergo sum*" ("I think, therefore I am"). For Descartes the simple fact of being able to "think" or "be aware" is unequivocal proof that there is something independent inside us that is separate from the rest of the world (from our body) and therefore exists.

Descartes' statement is also essentially dualist since he is formulating an irreconcilable dichotomy between our consciousness and the rest of what exists (outside of us).

On the other hand, Eastern non-dualism (*advaita* in Sanskrit) advocates not separating the essence of anything into categories. That is to say, everything that exists in the universe—we humans along with our consciousnesses, as well as plants, stars, rocks, animals, spirits, God or the gods, etc.—are all constituents of the same essence.

In other words, God or the gods are not all-powerful but are present in everything. Technically, this statement does not entirely align with all the pantheistic traditions. According to Hinduism, Brahman is the essence of everything in the universe, and is therefore all-powerful.

No one has summed up the non-dualism and worldview of Eastern thinking better than Alan Watts did when he said: "You are a function of what the whole universe is doing in the same way that a wave is a function of what the whole ocean is doing."

In his book *Ethics*, Baruch Spinoza (1634–1677) expounded his metaphysics concept according to which the whole universe is formed by a single infinite, eternal substance. He calls this substance "Nature or God," in Latin: "*Deus sive Natura.*"

When Albert Einstein—who is also known for having been fond of reading books about Eastern philosophy, and for being an admirer of Spinoza—was asked if he believed in God, he replied:

"I believe in Spinoza's God, who reveals himself in the orderly harmony of what exists, not in a God who concerns himself with the fates and actions of human beings."

On another occasion, Einstein explained more about his *weltanschauung* (German for worldview):

"A human being is a part of the whole called by us universe, a part limited in time and space. He experiences himself, his thoughts and feelings as something separated from the rest, a kind of optical delusion of his consciousnesses. This delusion is a kind of prison for us, restricting us to our personal desires and to affection for a few persons nearest to us. Our task must be to free ourselves from this prison by widening our circle of compassion to embrace all living creatures and the whole of nature in its beauty."

Non-duality in general and a worldview that generally aligns with pantheism is something else Shinto has in common with other Eastern traditions.

My mind was conditioned during the first decades of my life to split the fields of science and religion. This opposition or tension between viewpoints is another of the characteristics of Western thinking (which perhaps began with the Enlightenment). Whereas, in the East, the opposites coexist and complement one another. According to Taoism, *yin* cannot exist without *yang*.

Meeting scientists who were leading research groups at the University of Tokyo at the same time as they were working as monks in Buddhist temples or Shintoist shrines helped me to begin to see that things are not mutually exclusive. Both science and religion are part of the human experience.

Mythology, folk tales and sacred texts contain many truths and moral lessons that are more pragmatic and applicable to our lives than knowing Maxwell's equations. Even the most "rational" people among us act on the basis of beliefs; we don't calculate the forces involved using Newton's equations before sitting down on a chair. We simply hold the "belief" that the chair is not going to break.

"Superstitions appeal to our hopes as well as our fears. They often meet and gratify the inmost longings of the heart.

They offer certainties where reason can only afford possibilities or probabilities."

— Lafcadio Hearn, *Glimpses of Unfamiliar Japan,* First Series (English Edition)

But of course it is important to distinguish whether or not something is true from an epistemological point of view. With the advance of human science and technology, we no longer believe that the gods decide what the weather will be like tomorrow.

Ray Bradbury put it like this: "Where mystery begins, theology takes over. Two sides of the same coin. We have to think about the unthinkable, which is what religion does, and science. Both try to figure out what the heck is going on. How did we get here? The two are tools. One to work with facts, one to take up where the mystery begins."

So now, thanks to the Japanese, to Asia and the books I have read over the years, I appreciate the value both of science and of Eastern and Western religions and philosophies.

I think it is important to study whether or not traditions that have been with us for thousands of years are of benefit to humanity. The Lindy Effect, defined by Nassim Taleb, states that what does not disappear with the passing of time is "robust" and therefore has a certain usefulness for our survival. By contrast, there are other things that die out, for example, barbaric traditions such as child sacrifice in ancient Phoenicia, which disappeared over time. The Lindy Effect is a natural filter.

In Japan (generally speaking), technology, science, spirituality and millenary superstitions coexist in harmony. After two decades spent living here and having published ten books about Japanese culture, I am still learning new things about this rich and intricate civilization.

My desire to penetrate the halo of mystery surrounding Shinto led me to study its history, to converse with *mikos* (shrine maidens), *kanushis* (priests), carpenters specializing in shrine construction... The book you are holding in your hands is the result of what I have learned.

Shinto places more emphasis on actions (rituals, celebrations, visits to shrines...) than on a person identifying as a practitioner of a religion or on personal beliefs about nature or the world.

In comparison with other religions, rites are more important than beliefs.

Performing actions, and correctly carrying out each step of a ritual is more important than faith.

> *"I hear and I forget,*
> *I see and I remember,*
> *I do and I understand."*
> – Confucius

But even though I have been here for so long, certain types of behavior still surprise me. For example, I am still fascinated by the fact that Japanese CEOs (according to some surveys, over 90% of them), both at small businesses and big corporations, have a *kamidana* (a miniature Shintoist altar) in their office. Someone is entrusted with cleaning it and changing the rice and *sake* each day.

For a time, I was responsible for looking after the *kamidana* at the office where I worked. Each Monday, first thing in the morning, I would change the rice, *sake* and salt—I also used to wipe off the dust, following the instructions given to me by the previous custodian. One Monday, while I was cleaning the *kamidana*, the CEO walked past me and thanked me. And he added,

21

"It's very important in order for the company to do well." I asked him if he really believed the *kamidana* helped improve the company's sales and profits, to which he replied, "I don't know if it helps... but it certainly doesn't do us any harm. It's important to respect traditions."

Regardless of your beliefs, whether or not you believe in God, or in many gods, in life or the afterlife, or if you believe in reincarnation or not... this book's teachings will help you understand the traditions of Shinto. We shall concentrate on the actions, practice and history of this Japanese religion, which perhaps will serve to broaden your mind when it comes to the world's religions and the views of religion that you may have depending on the culture you come from.

This book is not intended to be a serious anthropology book—it is just a simple, entertaining introduction to Shinto and Japanese society and thinking.

In this book, I shall also leave aside epistemological truths, mixing mythology, fiction, beliefs, superstitions and historical facts. I will add notes wherever there is a record or proof of a historical truth. It is up to the reader to keep their mind open, to allow themselves to be swept along by their imagination and at the same time to probe into history in order to understand modern-day Japan.

> *"Science without religion is lame,*
> *and religion without science is blind."*
> – Albert Einstein

> *"Science cannot solve the ultimate mystery of nature. And that is because, in the last analysis, we ourselves are part of nature and therefore part of the mystery that we are trying to solve."*
> – Max Planck

The following table is a generalization, although there are exceptions, and in our increasingly globalized world the difference between both schools of thought is becoming less and less marked.

EASTERN THINKING	WESTERN THINKING
There are as many routes or paths to follow in life as there are living creatures.	Generally speaking, only a few routes to salvation exist.
Rituals are more important than beliefs.	Both beliefs and rituals are important.
Non-duality (the "self" and the universe or nature are manifestations of one and the same reality).	Duality (there is a separation between the "self" and the rest of the universe).
Belief in many gods (polytheism). Or that everything that exists is either a god or divine (pantheism).	Tendency to believe in one supreme being.
Collectivist.	Individualistic.
Opposites complement one another (*yin* and *yang*).	Tension between opposing visions.

Definitions of religion

Let me quote a reflection by Robin Dunbar in his book *How Religion Evolved: And Why It Endures*:

> "The definition of religion is probably the single most fiercely debated topic in the study of religion. Indeed, some scholars have even gone so far as to argue that the very concept of a religion is the product of the particular mindset that has characterized Western Europe since the Enlightenment. The Enlightenment, they argue, was dominated by a Christian dualist view that separates body and soul and draws a clear distinction between the earthly location where we humans live and the spiritual realm where God resides.
>
> In many small-scale ethnographic or tribal societies, the spiritual world is part of our world, not a separate world, spirits are embedded in every aspect of the environment. They share our world and are as corporeal and real as we are. We can study a particular culture's belief or ritual practices, but that's as far as we can go: we cannot really say how one culture's religion relates to another culture's because each culture views the world differently."

Robin Dunbar then goes on to explain:

> "There are the general views as to how religion has been defined. One derived from Emile Durkheim, asserts that a religion is a unified system of practices accepted by a moral community (a group of people who share a set of beliefs about the world). This takes an important anthropological view and emphasizes the important practical role that rituals and other practices play in most religions: **religion as something that people do**.

The other view takes a more philosophical or psychological approach: religion is a comprehensive worldview, a set of beliefs, that is accepted by a community as being true without need of evidence, **religion as something that a group of people believe."**

The part I have highlighted in bold is to emphasize that this is also one of the fundamental characteristics of Shinto.

A Shintoist Birth, a Christian Wedding, and a Buddhist Death

I love to visit shrines—they are almost endless. If I were to set out to visit one shrine a day, after a hundred years I still wouldn't have seen even half of the shrines there are in Japan! There are eighty thousand of them on record. And it is believed there may be just as many more that are not even registered.

Although they have elements in common, and are similar to one another, they all have slight differences that give them a special, unique personality. Visiting the local shrines wherever you travel in Japan is always a good idea.

According to data compiled in 2019 by the Japanese government's Agency for Cultural Affairs, 87,924,087 inhabitants of Japan consider themselves believers in or practitioners of Shintoist traditions.[3] At the same time, 83,971,139 follow Buddhist traditions, 1,915,294 Christian ones and finally 7,335,572 identify as followers of other religions. What's strange is that if we add up those numbers, we get 181,146,092 people. In total, over 181 million practitioners of religious traditions, which is much greater than the number of inhabitants, which stood at 126 million in 2019.

---

[3] Agency for Cultural Affairs (Government of Japan), *Shūkyō Nenkān Reiwa San-nenban,* https://www.bunka.go.jp/tokei_hakusho_shuppan/hakusho_nenji-hokokusho/shukyo_nenkan/pdf/r03nenkan.pdf

It is not an error of calculation or a contradiction; quite simply the majority of Japan's inhabitants practice both Shintoist and Buddhist traditions—they don't confine themselves to a single religion exclusively. In fact, many of them choose to celebrate their wedding with a Christian ceremony.

Although the majority do not identify with or adhere to any religion, it is also true that over recent decades sects based on "new religions" have proliferated and are gaining popularity.

A popular saying goes: "Born Shintoist, married like a Christian, and died like a Buddhist." It is a generalization, but a fairly accurate one. For example, according to statistics from the University of Yamagata, 90% of Japanese funerals are carried out following Buddhist ceremonies.[4]

My personal experience coincides with the stereotype. My wedding was celebrated in a Shintoist shrine and each year in early January my wife and I attend the *hatsumode* in Meiji Jingū; all the funerals I have attended were led by monks from Buddhist temples; at my in-laws' place there is a *kamidana* (Shinto) and a *butsudan* (Buddhism)—in the *butsudan* we offer food and incense to the family ancestors.

"Shinto is still, in a manner of speaking, the soul of Japan, and even young Westernized Japanese who take no part in its manifold ritual are conditioned, as their parents and grandparents were, by its fundamental characteristics."

— Shinichi Nagai

---

[4] Statistics from "Current Status and Research of Funeral Education in Japan" *Yamataga University Bulletin*, https://yamagata.repo.nii.ac.jp/records/1189

CHAPTER 1

Time Travelers

꧁ ✻ ꧂

"Hearing 100 times doesn't compare to seeing once."
– Japanese proverb

We Travel Back in Time Two Thousand Years—the Yayoi Period

We Witness an Animistic Ritual

Imagine we board a time machine and travel two thousand years back in time, to the Yayoi Period. We reach someplace on the island chain that in the future will be unified and become what we know as Japan. In the Yayoi Period, these are territories inhabited by tribes who mainly live off agriculture, fishing and hunting.

YAYOI PERIOD 300 BCE–300 CE	• First historical indications of religious activity. • Considered the era in which the first Shintoist beliefs and rituals emerged. • Beginnings of rice growing.

We are welcomed to a village of farmers.

On our mission as time-traveling anthropologists we observe the villagers, trying to bother them as little as possible. We see how they take advantage of every last strip of terrain to grow rice, how on the mountain slopes they conscientiously take care of tiered terraces, which reach to the very edge of the forests, where the slope is so steep it is unsuitable for planting crops.

It is fascinating to see the degree of collaboration and how united the community is. They help one another and share water by building canals in such a way that everyone's crops—not just those with easy access to water—prosper.

One day, we are woken up by an uproar. There are several villagers arguing loudly next to one of the rice fields on the edge of the woods. It appears that during the night some wild boars destroyed the plantation. One of the villagers is reminding the others that losing the harvest from one of the fields can mean going hungry during the winter. They cannot allow themselves to lose more. Someone has to go and hunt the wild boars to stop them from returning. Several youths set off equipped with bows and arrows and follow the boars' tracks—we lose sight of them when they enter the forest on the hillside.

Some of the elders prepare a few *sakaki* (*Cleyera japonica*) branches and *shimenawa*—a rope made of rice straw. They tie the rope around a rock, which is located between the destroyed rice field and the edge of the forest where the boars' tracks disappear among the undergrowth.

Sakaki 榊 *Cleyera japonica*

The *sakaki* is an evergreen tree native to warm areas of China, Korea and Japan. Along with the *hinoki* (Japanese cypress) it is considered to be a sacred tree. The *sakaki's* branches are used to mark out an object or sacred space, as an ornament, and also to make *tamagushi* (tool made with *sakaki* and bits of paper used in rituals).

In *The Chronicles of Japan* (*Nihon Shoki*, written in the eighth century CE), the *sakaki* is mentioned multiple times. According to mythology, the sun goddess Amaterasu became angry with her brother after an argument and shut herself away in a cave.

When she concealed herself, the light vanished from the world.

Faced with such a problem, several gods decorated a *sakaki* tree (with 500 branches) at the cave entrance with the aim of drawing Amaterasu's attention and getting her to come out.

Next, they carry out a ritual: they dance around the rock waving the *sakaki* branches and ask the *kami* for protection so that the rice fields will not suffer misfortune again.

A woman dances more energetically than the rest, entering into a kind of trance, her body contorting in impossible ways. Her eyes are glazed over and she pronounces incomprehensible words that appear to come out of her torso rather than her mouth. It reminds us of the medium from the movie *Rashōmon* (Akira Kurosawa, 1950).

When they finish, they tie the *sakaki* branches around the rock.

They also place several heaps of salt in the area bordering the woods, with the aim of repelling the wild boar.

Sacred salt

Shinto considers salt to be sacred. It represents cleanliness and purity. When *harae* or *harai* (purification) rituals are carried out, salt is often sprinkled over people. Piles of it are also often placed on saucers at the entrance to shops, restaurants and homes (盛り塩, *morishio*) to prevent evil spirits from entering. Sumo wrestlers also sprinkle salt in the ring before starting to fight.

It is odd that certain superstitions have survived the passing of time because they are of some use even though they arose before there was any scientific evidence of their effectiveness. Not knowing the reason why something works does not necessarily mean it is not effective. For example, the use of salt as a disinfectant has been a well-known custom around the world for thousands of years.

With the arrival of modern science, we know that salt is effective at killing bacteria. Nowadays, we also know that both pigs and wild boar can die of dehydration if they ingest too much salt.

"Shinto is more than religious faith. It is an amalgam of attitudes, ideas, and ways of doing things that through two millenniums and more have become an integral part of the way of Japanese people."

– Sokyo Ono

Historical notes from the Yayoi Period

In this first (time-traveling) chapter, almost everything is a product of my imagination, but I have tried to abide by facts we know about the Japanese islands' past to make the stories feasible.

Here is a list of things we know about the territory of Japan in the Yayoi Period (around two thousand years ago):

- Life mainly revolved around small villages, and when problems arose in the community, the *kami* were asked for help, by performing rituals around the *yorishiro*, which could be rocks, trees or even objects (mirrors, swords).
- Shinto in its current form did not yet exist, but there is historical evidence that rituals were already being practiced with natural elements such as tree branches and rocks.
- We know that as early as the second and third century BCE, belief systems and superstitions existed, mostly "animistic" ones, which evolved over time until they gave rise to Shinto.
- The superstition that salt is capable of purifying or repelling evil spirits is still extremely widespread to this very day. For example, in some shops or restaurants, piles of salt are positioned on plates at both sides of the doors.
- People hunted with a bow and arrow, and rice growing was one of the most common means of subsistence.

Yorishiro

The young hunters return triumphantly, bringing with them the bodies of three wild boar. All the villagers come together and carry out a purification ritual, dancing around the animals. After finishing the purification, we celebrate by eating a moonlit meal by the light of a campfire. We drink *sake* and gorge on wild boar meat—it is almost as though everyone has already forgotten the damage caused by the beasts.

Before going to sleep in one of the straw-roofed wooden houses we turn our gaze to the rock encircled by the *shimenawa* rope and the *sakaki* branches.

The rock has transformed into an object capable both of attracting the attention of the *kami* and of being inhabited by them. Over time, this type of rock would come to be known as *yorishiro* (依代).

The *yorishiro* could be considered one of the most primeval versions of what in time evolved into a Shintoist shrine. A *yorishiro* is an object that is capable of catching the eye of the *kami* and drawing them in. Through rituals or ceremonies, the *kami* are invited to "occupy the space" of the object, which is usually something natural like a rock or a tree.

This rock encircled by a *shimenawa* rope is a *yorishiro*.
In this case the rope is adorned with paper *shide*. Encrusted
in the center of the rock there is a sculpture of a sword.
(Photograph taken in Katori Jinja in the Kameido neighborhood, Tokyo).

When the concept of anthropomorphic deities had yet to permeate Japanese culture, any natural element or event was considered to be charged with spiritual power. Any living organism or inert object possesses energy (気: *ki*), and that energy is interconnected.

In the *Dragon Ball* (Akira Toriyama) manga and anime many of the techniques the characters use are based on the use of *ki*. One of the most powerful is the *genkidama* (元気玉: *ki* energy ball). In order to create this ball, Son Goku invokes all the living creatures from a planet or solar system. He asks each of them for a little *ki* in order to create a great ball of energy. Only a person with a pure heart can carry out this technique.

The sky, stones, sea, wind and mountains are all imbued with this *ki* energy. Trees, plants and animals also have this *ki* energy, and of course so do we humans.

Both *ki* and *kami* may be good or evil and they flow, traveling from one place to another, sometimes deciding to inhabit a living creature or an object for more time.

If a *kami* inhabits a *yorishiro* permanently or semi-permanently, it is then considered to be a *shintai*.

What is animism?

Animism is the belief that objects, natural elements, places and creatures have a spiritual essence.

Most religions evolved from animistic origins.

We know that from the Middle Paleolithic, human beings began to bury their dead following rituals and we started to create artifacts that were solely symbolic. The human brain began to have the capacity to have beliefs and superstitions.

These days, there are still many indigenous cultures with animistic belief systems, but they don't use the terms "religion" or "animism" to refer to their practices. They simply practice customs that are considered "animistic."

The term animism was introduced and developed by the anthropologist Sir Edward Tylor in his book *Primitive Culture* (1871). After studying and comparing the religious practices of many peoples around the world, he defined animism as "the general doctrine of souls and other spiritual beings in general... an idea of pervading life and will in nature." In other words, not only do human beings have a soul inside them, but all natural objects have a spiritual component.

Many religions have changed through history, abandoning their animistic background; on the other hand, others such as Shinto, Taoism and different kinds of Shamanism have clearly retained their animistic essence.

Superstitions and beliefs appear to be a universal part of human experience. They can be observed in any culture and throughout the entire course of history. In the book *Wired for God*, Charles Foster delves into the biology and neuroscience of this phenomenon. There are many signs that appear to indicate there is something coded into our biology that imbues us with the capability to have mystical experiences, enter into a trance or ecstasy and to tend to believe in supernatural entities and hold superstitions. We also tend to perform dances, ceremonies, rituals and have different ways of meditating or praying.

This may all be a mechanism to help us to survive. For example, believing that evil spirits roam the woods at night helps us to be afraid when we go into a forest at night. Hence the proliferation of tales, legends and stories, both in the West and in the East, in which the moral of the story is that we shouldn't go into a forest alone at night.

Richard Dawkins, author of *The God Delusion*, is one of the world's best-known atheists, but admits that he understands the irrational fear—feeling the presence of supernatural entities—that we humans may feel in certain situations. In an interview Richard Dawkins said:

> "I've certainly done that sort of thing—not stepping on the cracks in the paving stones or having to get over a certain line before the door slams behind me. I suspect it's extremely widespread and I could imagine it becoming quite dominating if I didn't have the armament of rational thought. Even then, I could imagine being frightened of spending the night in a notoriously haunted house, although rationally I don't believe in ghosts. Yes, these irrational fears are curious. They are part of our biology, aren't they?"[5]

---

[5] Richard Dawkins quoted in "The Man Who Feuded With God" by John Preston, *The Sydney Morning Herald,* https://www.smh.com.au/entertainment/books/the-man-who-feuded-with-god-20061222-gdp3k6.html

Kodama—Hayao Miyazaki's *Princess Mononoke*

One Japanese animistic belief is that spirits called *kodama* (木霊, 木魂 or 木魅) live in trees. The term is also used to refer to the tree in which the spirit lives. They are mentioned in the *Kojiki* (712 BCE), and in the *Genji Monogatari* (~712 BCE); in these manuscripts they are described as supernatural beings or spirits (*yokai*).

Japanese folklore has many fables in which an absent-minded person cuts down a tree where a *kodama* lives and a curse falls upon them. The older the tree is, the more likely it is to be inhabited by a *kodama*.

Normally, centennial trees, or those in which a *kodama* is believed to live, are marked with *shimenawa* ropes to prevent anyone from chopping them down.

Kodama appear in the movie *Princess Mononoke* (*Mononoke Hime*, 1997) by Hayao Miyazaki. The Japanese director decided to give the *kodama* a less humanoid and more abstract shape—he depicts them as big-headed dwarves that live among the branches of the forest trees. They move their heads in a strange way and give off hypnotic sounds.

Kodama also appear in several of the *Zelda* series of video games, where they have enormous heads and bodies like rag dolls.

Drawing of the apparition of a *kodama* in the book *Gazu Hyakki Yagyō* by Toriyama Sekein, published *in 1776*.

Wild boar and good and evil in Hayao Miyazaki's *Princess Mononoke*

In the Hayao Miyazaki movie *Princess Mononoke*, as well as *kodama*, the figure of a wild boar also appears and causes terror in a small village. The beast is possessed by an evil spirit that destroys everything it comes across.

At the beginning of the movie, Prince Ashitaka uses a bow and arrow to kill the boar. At that point, the evil spirit escapes from the animal's corpse but leaves a dark mark on the young prince's arm.

Upon observing the boar's lifeless body, and extracting an iron ball from it, they realize that in reality it was a benevolent *kami* called Nago.

The boar was neither good nor evil *per se*, but "contaminated" by an evil spirit. Shinto considers good and evil to be relative to the purity of the spirits that possess it.

If something is corrupted by an evil spirit it becomes evil. But it has the chance to become good again if it is purified.

In *Princess Mononoke*, the curse is transferred from the boar to Prince Ashitaka's arm. The village elders explain to the prince that the black stain will spread throughout his whole body transforming him into an evil being and that his death is inevitable. One of the elders suggests that if he travels in search of the source of the black ball he might have the chance to purify himself.

Shintai

The following day, we take our leave of the villagers and set off for the south. We are still in the Yayoi Period and we travel on horseback toward the lands that correspond to current-day Nara.

At sunset we reach our destination—Mount Miwa emerges on the horizon before us. Its triangular silhouette, blanketed by a verdant forest, looms over the great plain we are riding across. Mount Miwa is one of Japan's first sacred mountains. The *kami* Ōmononushi dwells there.

We come across a group of hundreds of workers who are digging and moving rocks. We get off our horses and the person in charge welcomes us.

He tells us they chose the site because it is near to Mount Miwa and so will be under its protection. He explains to us that they are building a tomb to honor Princess Yamato Totohi Momoso-hime.

We know that in the future this place will be known as the burial mound of Hashitaka Kofun, and that it will be the first of the six great keyhole-shaped burial mounds that remain in Japan.

This is how the book *The Chronicles of Japan* (*Nihon Shoki*) tells the story:

"The tombs were made by man by day and by God by night. During the day, the tombs were made by carrying stones from Mount Miwa. People lined up in rows from the mountain to the tombs, handing them over. The people of the time sang. 'If we pass over the stone mounds that we have inherited in Osaka with our hands, we may pass over them.'"

When a *kami* lives on a mountain, as is the case with Mount Miwa, it is considered to be a *shintai*, and villages, towns, cemeteries, shrines, temples, etc. flourish around it.

Shintai or *go-shintai*, are physical entities inhabited by *kami*. They are worshipped, yet are not considered gods, but rather vessels where the *kami* live permanently or semi-permanently.

Mount Fuji is the most famous *shintai* in Japan. It is said Princess Kono Hana Sakuya lives inside the volcano. When I climbed Mount Fuji, I was really surprised to see lots of Shintoist shrines devoted to Princess Kono Hana Sakuya—both at the foot of the mountain and at the summit. I later learned it was a sacred place and that traditionally only pilgrims were authorized to climb to the summit.

There are several types of *shintai*; they can be artificial objects such as mirrors, swords or jewelry. They can also be natural elements like rocks (*shin-ishi*), mountains (*shintai-zan* or *kanna-bi*), and waterfalls (*shin-taki*) or trees (*shin-boku*).

Totoro—*shinboku* trees

A *shinboku* (神木) is a tree or a forest worshipped as a *shintai*. That means, a *kami* is inside the tree. They are easily distinguished since they are encircled by a *shimenawa* rope.

In the movie *My Neighbor Totoro* (Hayao Miyazaki, 1988) a university professor moves to a country house with his two daughters Satsuki and Mei. The house is surrounded by a forest and the girls soon begin to notice that mysterious creatures dwell in it.

One day, Mei follows what looks like a white rabbit and it leads her to a hole in a giant tree inhabited by Totoro.

Totoro is a *kami* who lives in the sacred tree and is the protector of the forest. On seeing that Satsuki and Mei have good intentions and treat the forest well, he decides to help them. Those who have a corrupt spirit cannot find or see Totoro. Shinto says that only good-hearted people are favored by the *kami*.

One of the movie's messages is that we must treat the forest well—otherwise the *kami* who live in them will perish and stop helping humanity. This is a recurring theme in many Studio Ghibli movies, which are undoubtedly inspired by Shinto.

The forests are the source of life. If the relationships between humanity and nature break down, the forests will perish.

There are various ways of writing the word "forest" in Japanese. One of them is *mori* 森, and it turns out the word "protector" is also pronounced *o-mamori* お守. The word *chinju* 鎮守 (sacred forest) also contains the protection character 守.

Another ancient way of writing *mori* is 杜 or 社, which happens to correspond to the second character of the word *jinja* 神社 (Shintoist shrine). That is to say, one interpretation of the origin of the word *jinja* could be "forest of the *kami*."

The place where Totoro lives is a *chinju*, a forest that at the same time is a shrine where spirits reside. One of the best-known *chinju* is Meiji Jingū in Tokyo.

Himorogi

After walking all the way around the building zone, the foreman takes us to the slope of Mount Miwa.

There, clearly proud of himself, he shows us a *himorogi*. He explains they built it too. It is a very simple structure: a few poles linked by ropes forming a square boundary. Inside there is only gravel. The ropes sway rhythmically in a light breeze. We are enveloped by the rustling of tree leaves coming from the forest that covers the sacred mountain.

Himorogi (神籬) literally means "divine fence." The simplest *himorogi* is made by hammering four poles into the ground, which are tied together, thereby forming a square. The poles are usually made of bamboo or *sakaki* and the rope is traditionally woven using rice straw.

Within the area marked out by the *himorogi* there is normally gravel or different-sized stones. Sometimes the ropes are adorned with pieces of paper called *shide*.

The construction of a *himorogi* is a method of creating a safe, habitable place for the *kami*. Ceremonies and rituals are performed around it to invite them to go through the "divine fence."

If branches from a *sakaki* or from a small tree are placed in the center, they will act as a *yorishiro* and the *kami* will be able to live in them.

Himorogi in the Tsurugaoka Hachimangu shrine (Kamakura)

In terms of the evolution of the Shintoist shrine, we can consider the *himorogi* to predate the *jinja* (shrines). The idea of demarcating a divine area is immediately visible in them, even if it is with something as rudimentary as placing poles linked by ropes that symbolize the limit separating two worlds.

Later on, the limit between worlds would be marked out with wooden fences (*tamagaki*) and *torii* gates.

Akira Kurosawa's *Rashōmon*

Rashōmon, a movie from the year 1950 directed by Akira Kurosawa, is set in the Heian Period. One of the film's most important locations is the Rashōmon gate, which in ancient times was the main southern entrance to the capital Heian-kyō (current-day Kyoto).

One of the characters is a *miko* (Shintoist shrine maiden) who goes into a trance and can communicate with the ghost of a murdered samurai.

In order for the dead man to communicate through her, the *miko* (played by Noriko Honma) dances in front of a very simple *himorogi*. It has four *sakaki* branches stuck into the gravel ground linked by ropes enclosing a small white table on which there is a plate holding the ashes of the dead samurai.

She circles the *himorogi* shaking a kind of "magic wand" with bells (item used in *kagura* dancing) until she enters into a trance.

Possessed *miko*, or ones who have been converted into witches, are a recurring theme in Japanese tales and movies.

Scene from the movie *Rashōmon*.

We Travel to the Year 607 CE—
the Asuka Period

Prince Shōtoku — Arrival of Buddhism

Our next trip takes us to witness the beginnings of Japan as a unified country and the arrival of Buddhism in its territories.

We abandon the Mount Miwa area and hitch a ride on the time machine leaving the Yayoi Period behind to jump forward to the Asuka Period.

Our time machine lands in the Toyura-no-miya palace (in the modern-day Nara prefecture). The site's architecture, with a great gatehouse to the south side leading to a rectangular walled courtyard, recalls the structure of the Lost City of Beijing that we know from our trips in the present.

During the Asuka Period, Chinese culture began its expansion in the Japanese archipelago, influencing palace architecture, city structure, administration, government and laws. It was also the era in which Buddhism came to Japan. As time went by, through a process of syncretism the original beliefs and rituals of Shinto gradually merged with the ideas of Buddhism (in Chapter 8, we shall examine this aspect in more detail).

ASUKA
PERIOD
552 CE to 710 CE

- Arrival of Buddhism. Buddhist temples start to spread throughout Japan.
- Chinese architecture.
- Asuka is the imperial capital (modern-day Nara prefecture).
- Japan starts to be known as Nihon 日本 (the land of the rising sun).

Prince Shōtoku is considered to be a key historical figure in the spreading both of Confucianist and Buddhist ideas.

We cross the south courtyard and pass through another gateway into the northern complex, where we eventually come to

Prince Shōtoku's chambers. We are welcomed by his courtiers and have the great privilege of being able to speak with him.

We kneel down on cushions on the throne room *tatami* and Prince Shōtoku talks to us proudly about his knowledge of Buddhism.

(Prince Shōtoku [574–622] served Empress Suiko and is considered a key figure in the history of Japan due to his active involvement in the modernization of the government. He established a system of court ranks (imitating the government organization of China's Sui dynasty), and also promulgated what some people consider to be the first constitution of Japan.)

We ask him about his correspondence with China's Sui dynasty. When he sees we know about his interchange of letters with Emperor Yang, he looks at us in surprise. We tell him we are not spies, we simply come from the future and have read about his life in history books.

Prince Shōtoku unfurls the letter he received in the year 605 on the *tatami* floor. At the beginning of the parchment, we read, "the sovereign Sui government respectfully asks the sovereign Wa government…" He also shows us the letter of reply he has yet to send; in it, Prince Shōtoku has written, "From the sovereign government of the Land of the Rising Sun (*hi izuru tokoro* 日出るところ) to the sovereign government of the Land where the Sun Sets."

We are witnessing the first mention of the name Japan. In time, *Hi Izuru Tokoro* 日出るところ (literally, "place where the sun rises") would come to be pronounced "Nihon" 日本 and overseas it would be known as Japan, Nippon, Japonia etc.

Suddenly, Ono no Imoko comes into the chamber. Prince Shōtoku gives him the parchment with the reply and orders him to leave for the Sui dynasty in China and to deliver it to Emperor Yang.

Prince Shōtoku—historical notes

This account of our time machine trip to Prince Shōtoku's chambers is based on historical facts. The correspondence between Prince Shōtoku and Emperor Yang has been preserved. Prince Shōtoku received the letter in the year 605, and Ono no Imoko was the one who traveled with the reply "From the sovereign government of the Land of the Rising Sun (*Hi Izuru Tokoro* 日出るところ) to the sovereign government of the Land Where the Sun Sets" in the year 607 and handed it personally to Emperor Yang of the Sui empire (roughly corresponding to the eastern half of modern-day China).

A seventeen-article constitution (十七条憲法, *jūshichijō kenpō*) is mentioned in the *Chronicles of Japan* (*Nihon Shoki*). The document was written by Prince Shōtoku in the year 604. It differs from a modern constitution in that it focuses on listing a series of virtues rather than formulating basic laws and principles by which to rule:

First article: *wa* (和: harmony and peace) must be considered to be above all else.
Second article: belief in Buddhism prevails over the authority of the emperor.

The first article lays the foundations of what today can still be considered one of the bases of Japanese culture. Harmony or having good relations between companies when doing business, is often more highly valued than economic benefit. Another oft given example is that Japan is one of the countries with the fewest lawsuits per inhabitant.

The second article marks the official beginning of Buddhism's expansion; it arrived a little before this constitution was established (in the sixth century CE). Prince Shōtoku was a devout Buddhist who encouraged temple building and sutras written by him have been preserved. Legend also has it that he met Daruma in person.

Buddhist traditions, philosophy and beliefs spread through his territories over the following centuries while coexisting with local Shintoist beliefs, which were also beginning to take shape. Buddhist and Shintoist syncretism was on the rise in the twelfth and thirteenth centuries, a period in which Shintoist and Buddhist elements were merging in temples.

We Travel to the Year 1000 CE— Late Heian Period

Our next trip through time takes us to the tenth century.

We appear on the streets of Heian-kyō 平安京 (name of Kyoto in ancient times), one of the most highly populated cities in the world during that period.

Its streets are organized in a gridiron shape, an obvious legacy of the city structure of imperial China.

We walk along the magnificent Suzaku boulevard, where we find merchants, craftsmen, peasants selling vegetables, fishmongers, hunters…

HEIAN PERIOD
794–1185 CE

- During this era the capital is Heian-kyō (modern day Kyoto).
- Heian means "peace and harmony" in Japanese.
- Great influence of Chinese culture.
- Buddhism continues to boom in all of Japan's provinces.

The Torii *Gate*

In the boulevard we meet a carpenter, who has been entrusted with building a *torii* gate (鳥居). He tells us he has experience building entrance gates for Buddhist temples, but this is the first time he has faced the challenge of creating one for a Shintoist shrine.

45

Historians concur that the construction of *torii* gates and their use at the entrance to Shintoist shrines and also in Buddhist temples (since it was a time of coevolution for both religions) started to become rather commonplace from the start of the Heian Period. But given that most *torii* gates were built out of wood, it is difficult to know exactly how and when they appeared.

The first historic record of a *torii* gate is to be found in the book *The Inventory of the Properties of Ootori Jinja in Izumi*[6] (dated 922). Unfortunately, this *torii* gate is no longer standing.

The oldest surviving *torii* today is made of stone and is in the Hachiman shrine in Yamagata; it is known to have been constructed between the years 1086 and 1184 CE.[7]

The oldest surviving wooden one is built in the *ryōbu* style and is to be found in the Kubō Hachiman shrine in Yamanashi. It was built in the year 1535 CE.[8]

We may assume that in the period when we met the carpenter, *torii* gates were starting to become a common architectural element in Japan.

The carpenter tells us he has to build a roofless entranceway—typically, the entrances to Buddhist temples were protected from the rain—using two pillars (*hashira* 柱) connected at the top by a lintel (*kasagi* 笠木). Equipped with our knowledge of the future we tell the carpenter that over time this type of gate will come to be known as *torii*. Interested by our knowledge of the future, he asks us for advice and we tell him he can reinforce the structure by adding a *nuki* (extra lintel) below the *kasagi*.

---

[6] *Izumi no Kuni Ōtori Jinja Ryū Kichō* Source: National Diet Library, https://iss.ndl.go.jp/books/R000000004-I2368694-00?ar=4e1f&locale=en

[7] Data of the oldest stone *torii* extracted from the database of the Agency for Cultural Affairs (Government of Japan), https://bunka.nii.ac.jp/heritages/detail/143878

[8] Data of the oldest wooden *torii* extracted from the database of the Agency for Cultural Affairs (Government of Japan), https://bunka.nii.ac.jp/heritages/detail/121684

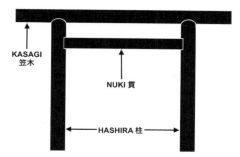

The most important elements of a *torii* gate are the two *hashira* (columns), the *kasagi* (lintel) and the *nuki* (reinforcement lintel).

Torii gates are sacred thresholds. They mark out the dividing line between the sacred world and the profane. This beautiful symbology is a recurring theme in Japanese manga, anime, novels and movies. When one of the characters passes through a doorway, they suddenly find themselves in another place or undergo a personal transformation.

These days they have become one of the most internationally recognized symbols of Japan. There is even a *torii* emoji character we can use on our smartphones and computers.

Engraving of a *torii* gate by Utagawa Hiroshige. (Famous Scenes of the Sixty Provinces, Bizen Province, Tanokuchi Coast, Yugasan Torii)

Ryōbu' style *torii* (with extra strengthening in the base) on the coast of the Daijingū shrine in an engraving by Utagawa Hiroshige.

Types of Torii *Gates*

There are more than a dozen styles of *torii* gates—here are the four most distinguishable ones.

Style	Description
Shime *torii*	We can imagine that this was the first evolutionary step in the architecture of *torii* gates. It is simply made up of two wooden columns linked by a *shimenawa* rope and adorned with *shide* (pieces of paper folded into a zigzag shape). In Chapter 2, we shall explain the symbology of the *shimenawa* and *shide* in more detail.
Shinmei *torii*	A more fundamental style of *torii* gate made up of two columns, a lintel at the top (*kasagi*) into which the columns are inserted, and a lower lintel (*nuki*) inserted into the columns.

Kasuga *torii* 	This adds more lintels at the top along with supports at the base of the columns. In the center, connecting the upper and lower lintels, a board (*gakutsuka*) is added, which is sometimes adorned with a word or just the name of the shrine.
Hachiman *torii*	Almost the same as the Kasuga *torii* except for a few details. For example, the ends of the upper lintels are at an angle.

Torii *Gates: Liminality, and Personal Transformation*

"Preliminary" (from the Latin *līmen* (threshold)) is an adjective that means "belonging or relative to a threshold or entrance." "Liminality" is a neologism whose use has become widespread in the fields of anthropology and psychology. It is used to refer to a limit, both in a metaphorical sense and regarding something real and physical.

Liminality is the feeling of ambiguity mixed with a certain disorientation and even madness or temporary elation that we feel when going through a moment of transition in our life. When we leave something important behind and replace it with a new fundamental element that we have yet to assimilate.

We tend to feel "liminality" when we celebrate a rite of passage: when getting past adolescence and becoming independent, when we celebrate a wedding, when we move to a faraway place, or when getting over a serious illness. These are moments in our lives when our identity is reconfigured.

In the book *The Hero With a Thousand Faces* (1949), Joseph Campbell described the importance of rites of passage and their similarity to the narrative or argumentative arcs of fables, mythology, novels and theater throughout the history of humankind. The identity of a story's main character or hero/heroine changes as they cross "thresholds" that take them to an unknown world that they have never experienced in their everyday life. They will also have to pass a series of "tests" (encounters with internal or external enemies) that will help them to gradually internalize their personal transformation.

George Lucas drew on both Joseph Campbell's work and that of Akira Kurosawa to create *Star Wars* in the 1970s. Luke Skywalker crosses the "threshold" and then has a series of adventures in a world whose existence he had been unaware of up until then. On passing all the "tests" he returns to his "normal" life once again but he is no longer the same person.

In the early 1980s, the manga artist Akira Toriyama confessed in several interviews to being a big *Star Wars* fan. Soon afterwards, in 1984, he began to publish the manga *Dragon Ball*, in which we can clearly see the influence of Joseph Campbell's ideas (popularized by *Star Wars*). The lead character, Son Goku, is living alone in the mountains when suddenly Bulma arrives and convinces him to go search for the dragon balls. This encounter encourages Son Goku to cross "the threshold of the unknown," abandoning his normal life. A great adventure begins, which will change both him (the hero of the story) and many of the companions and enemies he will meet along the way.

The use of the word "liminality" has also spread on the Internet where it is used to refer to "liminal spaces." A liminal space is something that makes us feel disoriented or a little bit nervous or worried, in a similar way to when we are about to cross a bridge of no return or take an irreversible life decision.

Sacred places tend to be designed for us to feel transition or transformation.

The suggestion of liminality in architecture, through the use of combinations of different-sized entrances, exits, rooms and hallways is something that has been observable for thousands of years, in the constructions of Ancient Egypt, in cathedrals, churches and mosques around the world, or in temples in China and India.

Torii gates bestow liminality on Shintoist shrines.

When I catch sight of a *torii*, even if it is far away, I cannot help but make a detour toward it. On passing beneath a *torii* I notice a difference in my emotional state—nothing as intense as a rite of passage but it is palpable.

If we could quantify liminality Fushimi Inari Taisha, in the south of Kyoto, would undoubtedly be the most liminal place in Japan. In this shrine, corridors formed by thousands of *torii* gates lead off into the woods of Mount Inari—walking among them can be hypnotic.

Weathering With You

Weathering With You (天気の子: *Tenki no Ko*) is a movie from the year 2019 directed by Makoto Shinkai in which a *torii* gate on the rooftop of a building in Yoyogi serves as a portal to take us to another dimension. Hina, the main character, has the power to affect time. But when she goes too far using her powers, she provokes torrential rain in Tokyo.

The *torii* gate is a symbol that serves to transport us to an alternative world in which fantasy is possible.

The symbology of *torii* gates inspires my imagination. In the year 2022 I published a novel entitled *La Era de la Eternidad* (*The Age of Eternity*) in which the main character also travels between different worlds via a portal; in my novel, instead of a Shintoist gate, I used a Buddhist gate (門: *mon*).

Jinja 神社

After spending a few days in Heian (former name for Kyoto and the capital of Japan from the year 794 until 1868) helping the carpenter to construct a *torii* gate—the rumor goes around that we are great sages. We keep the fact we are time travelers secret, but even so we are invited to visit the imperial palace, where Emperor Daigo awaits us.

An entourage accompanies us to the palace along the Suzaku boulevard. At the entrance, we are joined by even more soldiers—bodyguards armed with *katanas*.

After crossing several courtyards, we finally come to a chamber where Emperor Daigo greets us. In our audience with him, Emperor Daigo explains to us that he has entrusted Fujiwara no Tadahira with the task of cataloging all the *jinja* (Shintoist shrines) of Japan. Then Fujiwara no Tadahira comes into the room and performs a kneeling bow.

Fujiwara no Tadahira tells us he has already been working for over ten years on the manuscript and has cataloged 2,000 *jinja*. He says that when he finishes this arduous task, he will call it *Engishiki* (延喜式).

We, who come from the future, know this will be the first official, historic catalog of *jinja* and that when published (in the year 927), it would list 2,861 *jinja*.

Emperor Daigo and Fujiwara no Tadahira are both surprised by the great number of *jinja* and the speed at which they are proliferating. We cannot avoid the temptation of telling them that this is only the beginning and in the future there will be more than 80,000 *jinja* in Japan.

They explain to us that one of the problems they are facing is how to classify them. "What do you gentlemen think? What can be classified as a *jinja* and what cannot?"

In general, places where one or more *kami* live are considered *jinja* and to that end there is a *honden* (本殿) in which the *kami* is enshrined. The *honden* is usually a wooden construction, but in some cases there might not be one. There is simply a tree, a mountain or a rock that carries out the same function as the *honden*. For example, the famous Meoto Iwa rocks in Ise are a *jinja* and are simply two rocks linked by a *shimenawa* rope. In the case of O-Miwa in Nara and Mount Fuji the *honden* is a mountain.

Other typical *jinja* elements are the *torii* gates and the *haiden* (halls of worship).

We explain to Fujikawara no Tadahira and Emperor Daigo that the subtleties of the definition of what is and isn't a *jinja* shrine will continue to be a point of contention in the future. We tell Fujikawara no Tadahira that his work is not in vain and it will go down in history and continue to be used in the future.

These days, the Jinja Honcho (Association of Shinto Shrines) is tasked with classifying and maintaining the legacy of Japan's Shintoist shrines.

The word *jinja* is written with the characters 神社 (神: *kami*, 社: grove, place) In other words, a literal translation would be "place of the *kami*." The word *jinja* appeared as far back as the year 759 CE in the historic manuscript *Manyoshu* 万葉集.

The importance of nature for Shinto is even present in the etymology of the word *jinja*. As well as "place," another ancient meaning of 社 is "forest," that is to say: "*kami* grove."

- *Jinja* is the most generic term for referring to any type of Shintoist shrine. But there are other prefixes and suffixes:
  - *Jingū* (神宮) indicates that the shrine is imperial, whether because an emperor is enshrined in it or because it is or was the property of the imperial family. For example: Meiji Jingū.
  - *Miya* (宮) is used for shrines that house a special *kami* or a member of the imperial family.
  - *Taisha* (大社) literally means "great shrine."

Evolution of Sacred Shintoist Structures

On our time travels we have had the chance to witness *in situ* the evolution of the structure of places that are sacred to Shinto.

First, at the Yayoi Period village, where we saw the use of a *yorishiro* to try to shake off the threat of wild boars. We then saw how the entire Mount Miwa was honored as a *shintai* and how a mausoleum was built near it. There, beside Mount Miwa, we also saw a *himorogi* (four stakes hammered into the ground forming a rectangle linked by *shimenawa* ropes).

Finally, on our last time jump, we met a carpenter responsible for building a *torii* gate for the entrance to a *jinja* (Shintoist shrine).

The following diagram is a summary of the above. The evolution did not take place in a linear fashion—in fact, to this very day there are still *yorishiro, shintai, himorogi* and *jinja*; for this reason, the diagram has arrows pointing up and down. In addition, they are not mutually exclusive; a *shintai* may be a *yorishiro* and be part of a *jinja*, and at the same time contain or be near a *himorogi*.

Yorishiro

The most primitive form of a natural element used to attract *kami*.
It is usually just a rock or a tree (*shinboku*).

↓ ↑

Shintai

Natural objects (mountains, trees, waterfalls, rivers) where a *kami* is thought to live.

↓ ↑

Himorogi

Simple structure with wooden poles linked by *shimenawa* ropes that demarcate a sacred, rectangular zone.

↓ ↑

Jinja

Shintoist shrine in its most common guise.
The sacred area is enclosed by *tamagaki* wooden fences (玉垣) and the entrances have *torii* gates (鳥居).
A *kami* or various *kami* live in the *honden* (本殿).

We Travel to the Year 1183—End of the Heian Period and Beginning of the Kamakura Period

We climb aboard the time machine once more and arrive in the year 1183, near the end of the Heian Period; it is the height of the Genpei War (1180 to 1185). The end of this civil war between the Taira and Minamoto clans marked the beginning of the Kamakura Period and the capital was moved from Heian (Kyoto) to Kamakura in the year 1185.

KAMAKURA PERIOD
1185–1333 CE

- The power and control of Japanese territories passes from the nobility to the military. The Emperors rule but the Shogun dominate and control society.
- Buddhism continues to gain adepts. New schools emerge marking the beginning of "new Buddhism," led by Dogen and Eisai (both of them journeyed to China in the twelfth century).
- Mongol invasions (1274 to 1281). Legend has it that Shintoist monks helped to defeat the Mongols by invoking the "divine wind" (*kamikaze*): several typhoons sank a large part of the Mongol fleet.

Kabura-ya

We alight from our time machine at the summit of Mount Tonamiyama, looking down on the Kurikara gorge in the Etchū province. From our position, we can see the Minamoto and Taira clan troops preparing for battle.

We know the Minamoto will win this decisive battle. And that thanks to this victory, history will favor the Minamoto, who will end up ruling Japan from the year 1185, giving rise to the Kamakura Period.

We hear far-off whistles. It is a sound that brings to mind firework rockets shooting skywards just before they explode.

As we turn our gaze to the archers in both camps, we realize it is coming from the *kabura-ya* arrows. They are round-pointed arrows, not designed to kill, but to ward off evil spirits and attract the assistance of good *kami*. It is also a way of warning the enemy an attack is imminent. In fact, one of the translations of *kabura-ya* is "signal arrow."

Honoring and respecting the *kami* is more important than catching the enemy by surprise.

We are witnessing one of the last battles in Japanese history where the ritual component was more important than winning or losing. Later on, wars would become more aggressive and the *kabura-ya* arrows would cease to be used.

Kabura-ya arrows are made of either deer horn or wood. The spherical tip usually has an individually carved hole. This factor, combined with the skill of the archer, makes the whistle of each arrow unique.

We see how the Minamoto and the Taira shoot more than a hundred *kabura-ya*[9] before commencing a ferocious battle.

The terrain is steep, and the Minamoto do everything they can to make it seem like they have a lot of soldiers (such as flying numerous clan banners), but in reality they only have around five thousand men. Their strategy consists of separating into small groups that attack from different flanks and challenge the Taira to individual duels. Even so, it is very hard for them to fight against the Taira's forty thousand soldiers.

The end of the battle seems like something out of a fantasy story, but it is a historically documented event.

From our favorable position on the mountain summit, we can see herds of ox with flaming horns descending the valley slopes and charging at the Taira army. This is a technique that General Minamoto no Yoshitaka learned from reading books about Tian Dan, a general from the Qi state in ancient China who used herds of ox to fight in battles.

The fiery-horned ox trample to death the vast majority of the Taira and those who survive are so terrified they flee back to Heian-kyō (Kyoto).

---

[9] Stephen Turnbull in *Battles of the Samurai*. Arms and Armour Press, 1987

Final scene from the Battle of the Genpei War at Kurikara Gorge, where we can see the ox with blazing horns charging at the Taira.

These days, *kabura-ya* arrows are still launched into the air in some Shintoist shrines during celebrations with the aim of driving away evil spirits. It is also typical to find arrows for sale in the shops that trade in charms at the entrance to shrines. They are usually bought to keep at home as a protective ornament. The different arrow types have different names: Hama Ya, Hama Yumi, or Azusa Yumi.

Back to the Present—Meiji Jingū in Tokyo, the Year 2025

We leave our adventures with the time machine and return to the present. We get on the Tokyo subway and get off at Meiji Jingumae Harajuku' Station to visit the Meiji Jingū shrine.

We go through the main *torii* gate and instead of heading for the *haiden* like most visitors do, we decide to explore the iris garden. This garden was one of Emperor Meiji and his empress's favorite places to go for a walk in the late nineteenth and early twentieth centuries. After the death of the emperor in 1912, the Japanese government decided to erect a shrine in his honor called Meiji Jingū (明治神宮) enclosing the iris garden area.

The Japanese iris flower (native to Japan and China) is beautiful but fragile, and many Japanese poets have been inspired by it. Its ephemeral nature helps to awaken the feeling of *mono no aware* (物の哀れ)—a pang of melancholy we feel when realizing that nothing is permanent. Time flies both for flowers and for the rest of us.

> *"Trembling,*
> *in the middle of the lawn,*
> *the irises blossom."*
> – Kobayashi Issa

The shrine was completed in November 1920. The year 2020, when the Tokyo Olympic Games were slated to be celebrated, was the hundredth anniversary of its inauguration. Now, in 2025 tourism is filling the sacred grounds once again.

I wonder what the emperor and empress would have felt walking through the same scenery over a hundred years ago, contemplating the intense violet color of the flowers.

We close our eyes and imagine colored stars floating in the sky. They slowly fall, embellishing the inner garden, adding brushstrokes of violet, purple and white to the greens of the landscape.

Have you ever felt dizzy when realizing how quickly time passes? You look back at the past and into the future and feel your heart shrink; you don't know what to hold on to in order to avoid falling into an abyss of existential anxiety. Several decades have gone swiftly by and you realize the remaining ones will also vanish and all that will remain will be memories similar to the ephemeral memory of the light from a candle that has just gone out.

Back to reality, we open our eyes—they are no longer stars but iris flowers. A few petals flutter away in a slight breeze.

We walk along footpaths until we reach the Kiyomasa fountain, which is said to be a "power spot" (パワースポット—a place with healing powers) connected by invisible energy lines to Mount Fuji. We crouch down to wash our hands in the healing water.

We leave the garden and plunge into a dense, lush forest; it is as though each tree is trying to stake its claim to being the most elegant. Dark moss covers the northern side of each tree trunk.

The 70-hectare forest that surrounds Meiji Jingū is one of Tokyo's most important green "lungs." You get the feeling it has always been there, but the one hundred thousand plus trees were planted by volunteers only as far back as the 1920s. Honda Seiroku directed the planting and drew up a long-term plan. According to him, the forest would reach its full glory after 150 years. For that reason, he chose trees that grow slowly and live for centuries: Japanese cedars, pines, Zelkovas, Ginkgo Bilobas, Hinoki…

Another of Honda Seiroku's objectives was that after the initial planting it should not be necessary to plant more trees in the future, since they would regenerate without human intervention, thus becoming an "eternal forest." This is one example of the long-term planning that characterizes many aspects of Japanese society.

For the time being, Honda Seiroku's vision is coming true—new trees have not been planted for over a hundred years and the forest is looking magnificent. What will it look like in the year 2070 when the 150 years referred to in its initial planning have gone by?

We enjoy the *shinrinyoku* (forest bathing)[10] until we come to the last *torii*, which provides access to the shrine's main complex. We contemplate the gate's wooden beams; the texture and color are similar to that of the tree trunks in the surrounding forest.

We then wash our hands in the *temizu-ya* following the steps indicated on a signboard (see Chapter 2) and go in.

The buildings we are now looking at are not the original ones that were built to commemorate the death of Emperor Meiji. Meiji Jingū was reduced to ashes by American B-29 bombers in 1945; interestingly, this happened just one day after the wed-

---

[10] Héctor García and Francesc Miralles in *Forest Bathing: the Rejuvenating Practice of Shinrin Yoku*. Tuttle Publishing, 2020.

ding of the filmmaker Akira Kurosawa took place here. In his autobiography *Something Like an Autobiography* he describes this episode as a stroke of luck whereby he escaped death.

The current iteration is a reconstruction that was finished in 1958. The same *nagare-zukuri* architectural style as in the original was used (see Chapter 4) and they used the same construction methods and materials: Japanese cypress and copper for the roofs and decorations.

If it was destroyed in the war, what exactly celebrated its hundredth anniversary in 2020?

The essence is that which transcends the passing of time.

Everything is cyclically renewed, no matter whether it is natural, like the forest and the flowers in the garden, or artificial, like the *torii* and the shrine buildings. But they are not abrupt renewals, rather they are subtle ones, taking care to keep the essence. This effect of "renewal retaining the essence" is something the keen observer will notice in many places in Japan, except for certain parts of Tokyo where modernity sweeps the past away.

The construction method, the map of the grounds, the structure and appearance of the buildings are the same now as a hundred years ago. Although the "ingredients" of Meiji Jingū are not exactly the same now as when it was inaugurated, the original aesthetic lines are still the same. The traditions and festivals celebrated here are also a hundred years old or more, given that they have been practiced as part of Shintoist tradition for thousands of years, long before Meiji Jingū was inaugurated.

Although it is renewed like a phoenix rising from the ashes, the essence endures. The ones who change are us, the generations of people who continue to visit the grounds.

"Very like leaves upon this earth are the generations of men—old leaves, cast on the ground by wind, young leaves the greening forest bears when spring comes in. So mortals pass; one generation flowers even as another dies away."

– Homer, *The Iliad*

Art and traditions are tools with which we humans can retain intergenerational wisdom. But we can also use them to establish constants with which to resist the passing of time, helping us to open breaches in the space-time continuum that allow us to discern fading sparkles in eternity. They allow us to time travel.

A shrine, a temple, a cathedral, a synagogue, or a mosque, are all works of art that contain human tradition and wisdom.

In the West, we tend to make imposing buildings and works of art with the aim that they'll stand the test of time. By contrast, in Japan, traditions and forms have a little more weight, perhaps because every so often earthquakes and natural disasters tend to destroy almost everything. Both are valid ways of trying to fight in vain with the implacable second law of thermodynamics.

At the end of our visit, we pass through the last *torii* gate and return to the hustle and bustle of the city, swallowed up by the crowds in Harajuku and Omotesando. We imagine how before becoming a paved road, Omotesando was a dirt track; the emperors would return to their palace along this route after a stroll around the iris garden in the late nineteenth century.

We realize the walk we have just done in the year 2025 has made us feel something similar to what we experienced on our time machine trips. You might say that if we travel around Japan, exploring forests, museums, Shintoist shrines and Buddhist temples, it is like we are time traveling. The setting makes us feel just like people who used to walk here centuries ago.

Literature, music, dances, theater, architecture, philosophy, and all the artistic disciplines in general establish constants of what it means to exist as a human, which are difficult to define with words. These constants have the power—if only momentarily—to make us leap into the plane of eternity.

What are your constants in life?

Which activities, people, places or values, help you integrate the past, the present and the future in one connecting thread?

What helps you have moments of connection with eternity?

"Any moment might be our last.
Everything is more beautiful because we're doomed.
You will never be lovelier than you are now.
We will never be here again."

— Homer, *The Iliad*

"What we do now echoes in eternity."

— Marcus Aurelius, *Meditations*

"There is nothing you can see
that is not a flower;
there is nothing you can think
that is not the moon."

— Matsuo Bashō

Visiting Meiji Jingū in Tokyo

Meiji Jingū is one of the most accessible Shintoist shrines in Tokyo. It is right there when you come out of the west exit at the Japan Railways Harajuku Station on the Yamanote Line. It also has entrances from Sangubashi Station (Odakyu Line) and from Yoyogi (Yamanote Line).

Access to the shrine is free, but admittance the iris garden with the Kiyomasa fountain described above requires an entrance fee and access is restricted depending on the time of year. The best thing to do is to inquire beforehand on the shrine website: https://www.meijijingu.or.jp/en/

The Meiji Jingū shrine is one of the most easily accessible sacred sites in Japan.

When did the word Shinto 神道 first come into use?

The word *Shinto* 神道 was not used until the eighth century. The introduction of the word was necessary to differentiate between the indigenous traditions and beliefs of Japan and imported ones such as Buddhism, Confucianism and Taoism.

The precise chronology of the birth of Shinto is difficult to establish. But we know that some of its practices and beliefs go back thousands of years. The oldest known *dogū* figures are from 13,000 years ago, which shows that the settlers of that time already had some kind of belief. Although the exact use and meaning of the *dogū* or *haniwa* figures is a point of contention among archaeologists and historians, they all agree that they had a protective function. We might say they are the origin of the *omamori* (protective talismans) that are sold today in Shintoist shrines.

The video game fans among you will enjoy collecting *haniwa* figures in the Nintendo® video game *Animal Crossing* (*Dōbustu no mori*).

The customs of the islands' first settlers gradually evolved, beginning with animism. But little by little, especially after the sixth century, they began to be influenced by the great Asian religions of the period: Buddhism, Taoism, and Confucianism. In the preceding phrase I used the word "influenced," but a more appropriate word might be "absorbed." One of the apparently atemporal aspects of Japanese society is its capacity to adapt what they import from overseas to their local customs. An example is the Japanese writing system, which was an adaptation of the one used in Chinese territories. Something more recent is the transistor radio, invented at Bell Labs in the United States in 1947, but exploited by Japanese multinationals in the 1970s and 1980s. The attentive traveler will observe this behavior in Japanese restaurants, which serve versions of western food with odd modifications.

After several centuries of Buddhist, Taoist and Confucian influence, the time came when it was hard to distinguish what was local from what was imported. That was the moment when it was decided to begin using the word "Shintō"; prior to that, there wasn't even a word to refer to local customs and beliefs—they were just practiced.

In this way, it started to be possible to differentiate between Shinto and Buddhism, but even today the two are intertwined together as if in a lovers' dance.

As we shall see throughout this book, the dividing lines between philosophies and religions in Japan are blurred since they have coexisted and influenced one another for centuries. Shinto in its current state would never have existed without Buddhism and vice versa.

"The nature of Shinto speaks to our human nature. Shinto speaks to us, to something in us which is deep and permanent."

– Donald Richie

CHAPTER 2

ELEMENTS AND SYMBOLS

ഓ✻ଔ

"A single arrow is easily broken, but not ten in a bundle." (一矢)
– Japanese proverb

Torii

Torii gates mark the entrance to Shintoist shrines and symbolize the transition to sacred territory. Most *torii* gates are made of wood, but there are also stone, concrete and metal ones. They are usually painted a reddish color and the upper lintel is sometimes black.

Some of the country's most photogenic shrines have an abundance of gates forming corridors. In this case the majority of *torii* are donations from nearby businesses and also from families and individuals who want to show their gratitude to the *kami*.

One of the simplest ways of differentiating between a Buddhist temple and a Shintoist shrine is to look out for *torii* gates, although there are a few exceptions, such as the Shitennō-ji temple in Osaka, which is Buddhist but has *torii* gates.

The *torii* gate has become one of Japan's most international symbols.

Ema

As a visitor to a shrine, you can purchase a wooden board *ema* (絵馬). The front part usually has a drawing related to the shrine. You also sometimes have the chance to choose the theme: love, good health, success in business or with your studies. On the back, you can write a wish and once you have done so, the traditional thing to do is to hang the board up. There is usually a designated place to hang them, normally near a sacred tree.

Ema boards are easy to spot thanks to their shape which is reminiscent of the outline of a house.

Shimenawa

Shimenawa are ropes made of (normally rice) straw, which are used to mark something sacred. They tend to be hung from the top of *torii* gates or around tree trunks or rocks. They are sometimes adorned with *shide*, pieces of paper folded into a zigzag shape (see next section).

One of the literal translations of *shimenawa* is "rope (*nawa*) that separates (*shime*)." In order to explain the origin of *shimenawa* ropes and their symbology as a tool for separating the sacred, we can turn to a legend that recounts how Amaterasu, the sun goddess, hid in a cave after fighting with her brother.

During her exile in the cave, the universe lost its shine.

Several *kami* persuaded Amaterasu to come out of the cave. That was when the *kami* Futodama placed a magic rope (*shimenawa*) between Amaterasu and the cave entrance to stop her from hiding there again.

Light returned to the universe.

The sun goddess Amaterasu coming out of the cave, as imagined by the artist Shunsai Toshimasa in the nineteenth century. Can you find the *shimenawa* rope?

Shimenawa rope linking the two Meoto Iwa rocks. Legend has it they represent the union of the creator gods Izanami and Izanagi.

A visit to the Amaterasu Cave

If you like to get off the beaten track, the cave from the legend of Amaterasu as narrated in the *Kojiki* is to be found in the Amano Iwato-jinja shrine (天岩戸神社).

It is in the Miyazaki prefecture in a remote location. To get there, you will need to take a bus from Nobeoka Station and get off at Miyako and then from Miyako take another bus to Iwato. The easiest thing to do is to hire a car and go directly to: 1073-1 Iwato, Takachiho, Nishiusuki District, Miyazaki 882–1621.

Entrance to the cave where legend has it the goddess Amaterasu hid after a squabble with her brother Susanoo. In the photo we can see the *shimenawa* rope hanging to mark the entrance to the sacred site as well as the *torii* gates.

68

Shide—Tamagushi, Gohei, Haraegushi

Shide are zigzag-shaped paper decorations. The length of them depends on the way they are folded, and they have a multitude of uses.

Shide are used:

1. As a decoration hanging from *shimenawa* ropes.

I took this photo on Mount Mitake at the Ayahiro waterfall. A *shimenawa* rope is hanging from the *torii* decorated with four *shide*. The waterfall is a popular place for practicing *takigyo* (bathing beneath the stream of a waterfall). In Chapter 5 we shall learn more details about water purification rituals.

2. When the *shide* are joined to *sakaki* branches, the term used is *tamagushi*. *Tamagushi* are important in wedding celebrations.

A *tamagushi* is a *sakaki* branch adorned with *shide*. Both simple and beautiful.

3. When it is a pole with just two *shide*, then it is a *gohei*. *Miko* "shrine maidens" use *gohei* in purification rituals. They are normally shaken from left to right above the object or person being subjected to purification.

A *gohei* may be identified by the fact it only has two hanging paper *shide*.

4. If a wooden pole is adorned with a multitude of *shide* it is known as an *ōnusa*, *nusa* or *taima*. These are used as a decoration and also in ceremonies and rituals. If it has a white-colored base, the correct term is *haraegushi*. These tools, which you may think look like magic wands, tend to be seen, among other occasions, in rituals carried out before beginning the construction of a new house or building (*jichinsai*) or when purchasing a new car.

When *ōnusa* are not being used, they are usually kept in the *honden* or *haiden*.

A *kannushi* (master of ceremonies) shaking a *haraegushi* over the engine of a new car carrying out a ritual called *kuruma-barai* (車祓い, whereby *kuruma* 車 means "car" or "automobile" and *barai* 祓い means "purification" or "cleaning"). It is believed to help prevent traffic accidents and breakdowns. In Chapter 5 we shall explore the meaning of *barai* or *harai* in more depth and its importance in Shinto.

Omikuji

Omikuji are strips of paper that tell your fortune. They are randomly chosen and contain predictions about your fortune that range from *daikichi* ("very lucky") to *daikyō* ("very unlucky"). Some people say they are the origin of the famous fortune cookies that are popular in Asian food restaurants in the United States and Canada.

In the event you have drawn bad luck, it is usual to tie the paper to a tree branch or a rope before leaving the grounds (there is a place designated for that). Symbolically, we are leaving the bad luck behind. If we get a good luck ticket, the custom is to keep it in our purse in order to carry good luck with us.

Omikuji paper strips come in a variety of styles with different features, but generally speaking they are a common element both in Shintoist shrines and Buddhist temples.

There is usually a designated place for hanging *omikuji*.
The paper is folded in such a way that it can be knotted around a rope.

Chozu-ya or Temizu-ya

Chozu-ya or *Temizu-ya* are fountains located at the entrance to shrines, normally coming after you have crossed through the main *torii* gate.

The correct way to purify oneself using the fountain water is:

1. Use one of the ladles to put water in one of your hands.
2. Bring the water from your hand to your mouth. Never drink straight from the ladle.
3. Spit the water out onto the ground. There is usually a pebbled area around the stone basin.

Two women using a *temizu-ya* fountain in the Meiji Period (1868–1912).

Hokora

Hokora (祠) or *Hokura* (神庫) are miniature shrines. They are to be found both within the grounds of other larger shrines and outside of them, in independent locations. Oftentimes they are found on paths or trails, where they are designed to protect travelers.

At the start of the movie *Spirited Away*, when the father takes a detour with the car and heads into a forest, the lead character sees several *hokora* in the shadow of the trees. This is the first sign they are about to cross into another dimension or magical world.

Some experts argue it was one of the first words in Japanese to refer to a shrine. *Hokura* (神庫), literally means *"kami* repository."

A *hokora* is a miniature shrine. They are usually found in mountains, forests, and at the edge of paths or trails.

Iwakura

Iwakura (岩倉) refers to the belief in rocks like *yorishiro* in which the *kami* live. These rocks are worshipped and are normally encircled by a *shimenawa* rope.

According to the Iwakura Association, which is dedicated to the investigation of the origins of artificial rock formations and megalithic structures, the beginnings of the manipulation of rocks to mark sacred paths or sites goes back to the Jōmon Period (13,000 BCE to 300 BCE).

Iwakura in Yama-no-kami (山ノ神) in the city of Sakurai (Nara prefecture)

Meoto-iwa are a subset of *iwakura* that are always in pairs linked
by a *shimenawa* rope. As stated on page 67, the two rocks
represent the union of the creator *kami*: Izanagi and Izanami.
They celebrate the marriage of man and woman.

Inari Foxes

Inari Ōkami is the *kami* of foxes (*kitsune*), of rice, fertility, agriculture and prosperity in general. It is one of the most popular *kami*; more than a third of the Shintoist shrines in Japan are devoted to Inari. It is easy to spot them thanks to their fox statues. Legend has it that foxes are messengers or avatars of Inari.

The statues often have a red-colored bib (*yodarekake*) hanging around their neck. The color red, sometimes in a tint closer to vermilion, is the most prevalent color in the shrines devoted to

Inari; he is believed to be capable of warding off evil spirits and of protecting us from illnesses.

Statue of a fox at the entrance to an Inari shrine.

Inari, Konkon, Koi Iroha

Inari, Konkon, Koi Iroha is the title of a manga series, which has been adapted to anime. At the beginning of the story, the character called Inari Fushimi, decides to try to find a shortcut to get to school. But on the way she gets distracted when she sees a fox cub fall into a river. She jumps in the river and swims toward the cub and saves it.

Uka-no-mitama-no-kami, one of the *kami* identified by Japanese mythology as Inari, is impressed by the girl's act and as a show of gratitude decides to bestow supernatural powers on her. With her new abilities, she can transform into other people.

The transformation of people (*henge* 変化) into other people, and of animals to people and vice versa, is typical of Japanese folk tales, movies and novels.

Fushimi Inari, the name of the main character, is the name of one of the most important shrines in Japan devoted to Inari.

Visiting the Fushimi Inari shrine

Fushimi Inari is one of the most visually spectacular shrines in Japan. Thousands of *torii* gates are lined up forming corridors that plunge into the mountain forest.

Many of the *torii* gates are donations. You can make a donation from as little as 400,000 yen to get a *torii* gate built with your name on it.

Shigeru Miyamoto, the designer of Nintendo video games who created *Super Mario Bros.* and *Donkey Kong* among others, has spoken about this shrine several times in interviews and about how it has given him ideas for his games. It was a direct source of inspiration for the creation of *Star Fox*, a spaceship game in which you have to traverse portals.[11]

How to get there: at Kyoto Station get on the Japan Railways Nara Line and stop at the second station, which is called JR Inari. From there it is just a few minutes on foot to the start of the uphill route to the *torii* gates.

One of the corridors of *torii* gates at the Fushimi Inari shrine.

[11] "Miyamoto Explains How He Turned His Love for a Japanese Shrine Into a Videogame" by Chris Priestman. *Killscreen*, June 18, 2015. https://killscreen.com/previously/articles/miyamoto-explains-turned-love-japanese-shrine-videogame/amp/

Komainu

Komainu (狛犬) are statues of dogs with lion-like features. Just as foxes can be seen at the entrance to shrines devoted to Inari, *komainu* statues serve as guards at shrines devoted to Hachiman, the god of war.

These guardian statues originate from China, and it is commonplace to come across them throughout most of Asia. In China they are known as *shishi* and in Korea as *haetae*. Some styles look more like lions and others more like dogs.

Their symbology is of Buddhist origin. One of the statues has its mouth open—*a-gyō* (阿形)—and we can imagine it pronouncing the syllable "a," while the other one's mouth is closed—*un-gyō* (吽形)—and we can imagine it pronouncing the syllable "un." Buddhist belief has it that these sounds have the power to ward off evil spirits.

Two stone *komainu*, one with its mouth open and the other closed, guarding a shrine.

Shinboku

Shinboku (神木) are trees or forests regarded as *shintai* (one or more *kami* dwell in them). They are usually encircled by a *shimenawa* rope.

Sacred *shinboku* tree in the mountains of Hakone.

Tengu

Tengu (天狗, 天: heaven or heavenly, 狗: dog, bird of prey or crow) are supernatural creatures of Japanese folklore and are worshipped both in Shinto and Buddhism.

They are humanoid beings with birdlike features: they have long beaks, and are winged and feathered. They are very strong, can fly and are also capable of being invisible. They are regarded as the custodians of forests and sacred mountains.

An outing to the *tengu* mountain—Mount Takao

It is typical to go on a day trip from Tokyo to Mount Takao, a beautiful mountain full of shrines and protected by the *tengu*.

Takao is only 50 minutes away by train from the center of Tokyo. To get there, you have to take the Keio Line at Shinjuku Station and go as far as Takaosanguchi Station. It is also possible to travel there on the JR Chuo Line changing trains at the end of the line.

On the climbing route, there are several temples and shrines on the way, along with lots of *tengu*, who are said to chase and attack any evil being.

From the summit, at an altitude of 599 meters (1965 feet), if the weather is good, you can see the outline of Mount Fuji on the horizon.

MYTHOLOGY

ℵ❊ℜ

*"At the time of the beginning of heaven and earth, there came into
existence in Takamanohara a deity named Ame-no-Minakanushi-no-
Kami; next, Takamimusubi-no-Kami; next, Kamimusubi-no-Kami.
These three deities all came into existence as single deities,
and their forms were not visible."*

– First phrase of the *Kojiki*, translated by Philippi, Donald L.

The *Kojiki* (*Records of Ancient Matters*) and the *Nihon Shoki* (*Chronicles of Japan*), compiled in the eighth century, are regarded as two of the most important documents in the history of Japan. Both collections of stories describe how the Japanese archipelago was born. They coincide regarding some myths but also differ on many points. The comparison of the *Kojiki* and the *Nihon Shoki* is a subject that has been written about at length by scholars and is still being studied today. A close examination of the *Kojiki* and the *Nihon Shoki* is beyond the scope of this book. For readers who are interested in the subject, I recommend the book *The Kojiki: Records of Ancient Matters* (Tuttle Classics).

The following is my simplified version of the cosmogeny of Japan, based primarily on the *Kojiki*.

The First Island Created by Izanami and Izanagi

Many eons ago…

The universe was made up of silence, darkness and a great mass of formless material. The particles contained in this great mass of *ame-tsuchi* (天地: heaven, earth) began to split up, to create light and to collide creating the first sounds ever heard. The movement of the material produced the clouds and the sky, where the first three *kami* in Japanese mythology spontaneously appeared: Ame-no-Minakanushi-no-Kami; Takamimusubi-no-Kami; Kami-musubi-no-Kami.

Below the sky, a great sphere was left made up of still unordered particles that the *kami* decided to call The Earth. After another seven generations of *kami,* the creators of Japan, the goddess Izanami and the god Izanagi were born.

The siblings Izanami and Izanagi were ordered to create a territory on The Earth. They accepted the responsibility and were given a sacred *naginata* (spear) called Amenonuhoko (天沼矛, spear of heaven and sea) that would help them to carry out their mission.

Brother and sister journeyed together and eventually landed on a floating bridge. Leaning down from it they churned the seawater with the tip of the Amenonuhoko spear. When they took the spear out of the sea, the drops of saltwater that remained on the tip condensed creating the first island of Japan: Onogorishima.

Kobayashi Eitaku's "Izanami and Izanagi Creating the Japanese Islands," can be seen on a hanging scroll at the Boston Museum of Fine Arts. Izanagi, the male deity, is depicted on the right holding the sacred Amenonuhoko, while Izanami, the female deity, is standing on the left. Together, they are stirring the primeval waters, breathing life into the islands of Japan. This myth is central to Shintoist mythology and is deeply entrenched in Japanese culture.

According to several historians, among them Motoori Norinaga, the mythical island of Onogorishima corresponds to someplace to the south of Awajishima (淡路島). The most popular candidate is Nushima, an island of barely 2.7 square kilometers (1 square mile) and 2,500 inhabitants. On this small island there is a shrine called Onogoro-jinja devoted to the myth of the creation of Japan and also a rock called Kamitategami-Iwa that recalls the outline of a spear tip.

The Kamitategami-iwa rock seen from the south of Nushima. This place is believed to correspond to the legendary island of Onogorishima, which is mentioned several times in the *Kojiki* (*Records of Ancient Matters*) as the place where Japan was born.

How to get to Nushima

Nushima is a small island barely 10 kilometers (6 miles) in circumference. The only point of interest here is the legend that suggests this is where Izanami and Izanagi decided to start to create the Japanese archipelago thrusting their spear into the sea.

The most interesting place is the Onogoro shrine, which has one of the biggest *torii* gates in Japan

The best way to get there is to go to the port of Nada (in Awajima) and from there take the ferry that goes directly to the port of Nushima. There are 10 crossings a day in each direction between Nada and Nushima, starting at 6.20 in the morning and finishing at 7 PM. Detailed timetable: http://nushima-yoshijin.jp/go_kisen

With the same spear they carried on with their labor and created Honshū, Shikoku and Kyushū… They also created forests, mountains and rivers. Finally, Izanami and Izanagi built themselves a house and got married. Yes, they were siblings, but they got married.

To continue with the task with which the other *kami* had entrusted them, they had many sons and daughters. Their offspring would continue to create and care for Japan. Thus were born the *kami* of the wind, the *kami* of the moon, the *kami* of the sea, the *kami* of the forests, the *kami* of the mountains…

But when Kagutsuchi—the *kami* of fire—was born, the flames he produced were so powerful they killed his mother Izanami. After this tragic event, his father Izanagi went wild and in a fit of rage cut off his son's head with his sword. This event marks the end of the creation myth.

Izanagi, saddened by the death of his wife, decides to journey to the netherworld (黄泉: *yomi*) to try to rescue her.

Izanagi in the Netherworld—Yomi

Izanagi managed to locate his wife in the *yomi* (netherworld) and spoke to her although he couldn't see her, due to the total darkness there.

"My darling, our creation of the world is unfinished—you have to return to finish what we started together," said Izanagi.

"I want to come with you, but I fear it is too late. I have already eaten food from this place... let me speak to the master of this world and see what he advises. Meanwhile, you wait here and whatever you do, don't look at me."

Izanagi waited patiently for a while but could not resist temptation and finally disobeyed. He broke off a piece of the comb he wore in his hair and improvised a torch with which he might see his wife. He made out a figure that did not seem human. His wife had become an abominable shapeless mass, covered in worms, maggots and bugs ...

"You've betrayed me, you've broken your promise! Shame on you, you've humiliated me! I ordered you not to look at me!" she said.

She then invoked a horde of *shikome* (ugly women from the netherworld, or demon women) to chase her husband, who ran away. As he escaped, he fought the *shikome* using grapes and peaches as weapons. Finally, he managed to escape from the netherworld.

It is strange that fruit appears as a powerful element that can even neutralize demon women. These days, fruit is still highly regarded in Japan. Peaches are sometimes sold individually: placed at the center of crates adorned with ribbons.

This *Zelkova serrata*, also called the Keyaki, is a *goshingi*—a shrine's sacred tree. Over a hundred of these trees line the approach to the shrine at Okunitama-jinja. The Keyaki has long been regarded as sacred—a guardian of the places and people surrounding it, a potential home for the *kami*. On the shrine premises, these trees are distinguished by their *shimenawa*, the sacred rope that wards off evil spirits and marks the dwellings of gods.

Torii gates can be found throughout a shrine complex and can vary in size, style and color. These traditional red but otherwise very simply-styled *torii* complete an approach to the shrine. Generally, the inscriptions on the posts are the names of donors.

In Shinto, a bath house, or *onsen*, is a center of community and a place to cleanse the soul as well as the body. In Miyazaki's *Spirited Away*, the bath house is the heart of the story's activity. This entry in a 2024 art exhibition celebrating this iconic film depicts the main players, overseen by the villainous Yubaba who, with her Western dress and accoutrements, represents the unhealthy influence of capitalism on the daily life and mindset of Japan.

Rituals and blessings come in all shapes and sizes, and they happen everywhere—at massive and elaborate public shrines, at homes and public buildings, and at small, private shrines were families gather for private rituals of purification, petition, renewal or gratitude. Here, a priest blesses a family gathered for a private ceremony.

Power tools are not used in the building of Shinto shrines. Similarly, whether a *dashi* (float) is the wheeled structure called a *hoku*, the structure on poles called the *yama*, or the small sacred palanquin called the *mikoshi*, in which the *kami* is transported, these structures are propelled entirely by human effort. Teams of community members push or carry these floats and shrines through the streets during *matsuri*—festivals celebrating the gods and offering thanks for their favor through the year.

Rustic *torii* line the approach to the mountains at Yahiko Jinja, Niigata Prefecture. The shrine's origins are said to extend back to 657 BCE with the arrival of Amenokaguyama no Mikoto, grandson of the sun goddess. Although the shrine buildings were destroyed by fire and rebuilt in the early 20th century, the *kami*'s shrine is housed safely within the mountain itself.

Many settings can be home to a shrine—urban landscapes, forests, mountains, the seaside. Each contributes something unique to the shrine's spiritual ethos. Udo Jingū in Miyazaki Prefecture is said to be the birthplace of Ugayafukiaezu, father of Emperor Jimmu, the first emperor of Japan according to the *Kojiki* and *Nihon Shoki*.

Patron of fishermen, farmers and merchants, and one of the Seven Lucky Gods, Ebisu is one of Japan's most active deities. Unlike his fellow lucky gods, whose origins are shared with Buddhism and Hinduism, Ebisu is Shinto to the core, giving him a special place in the hearts of the Japanese people. His festival occurs in the tenth month, called *Kannazuki*, the month without gods, so-called because that is the time when the divine host gathers at Izumo-taisha—except for Ebisu, who somehow missed the summons, leaving him free to be petitioned and celebrated.

Before construction begins on a new building a priest will perform a ritual called *Jichinsai* to bless the site and petition the *Jinushigami*—landlord deities— for the safe completion of the undertaking. Offerings of *omiki* (the libations), foods such as fish, rice, and produce, and of *tamagushi* (a branch of the *sakaki* tree, used in many different Shinto rituals) are made. The altar is set up on the site, and is attended by the building's owners, architects and builders.

Two *kannushi* (priests) and *miko* (shine maidens) prepare to lead a wedding procession. At one point during the ceremony, the *miko* will perform a ceremonial dance to please the gods and call their favor upon the bride and groom.

The use of the stone lantern has grown widely from its origins as a votive light in Buddhist temples. These lanterns—called *toro* are made of stone, wood or metal— have appeared in myriad styles since they were adopted by Shintoism during the Heian period. Here, they line the path at Hie-jinja.

The *temizu* ritual is performed before a visitor enters the shrine. The dipper is taken first in the right hand in order to wash the left, then is moved to the left in order to wash the right. The dipper is returned to the right hand and water is poured into the cupped left hand in order to rinse the mouth. Any remaining water is allowed to flow down the handle before the dipper is replaced.

Shinto priests, called *kannushi*, march into the shrine, a formation particularly common in preparation for major rituals, such as the welcoming of the new year, when the Japanese pull out all stops and celebrate as a nation. Here, a group of priests processes into Ise Jingū.

Founded in 586, Haruna-jinja is surrounded by majestic yet serene mountains, lakes and forests, creating a unique atmosphere of beauty and power. It is said to be home to the gods of fire, water, and agriculture. It has long been a place to seek blessings for world peace as well as for a good harvest, success in business and happiness in marriage.

Shinkyo Bridge crosses the river on Mount Haguro, one of the Dewa Sanzan (Three Mountains of Dewa). Beyond the bridge, 2446 steps lead to the shrine. Thousands upon thousands of pilgrims have crossed this bridge. At the end is the *chinowa kuguri*, the grass ring through which visitors pass to ward off evil. Like so many Japanese rituals, passing through the ring involves a series of steps that include bowing and walking in and out of the ring in a figure eight, left foot first.

At Fushimi Inari Taisha, preeminent among all of Japan's Inari shrines, Inari statues come in all shapes and sizes, and can be seen everywhere on the grounds. Inari is a patron god of many aspects of Japanese life, from rice cultivation to trading and selling. Small figurines like these serve as votive offerings to petition the god for success in these and other endeavors.

Once the site of the shrine Kumano Hongū Taisha, the sandbank forming the confluence of the Otonashi and Kumano rivers at Ōyunohara was flooded in 1889, and the shrine's buildings were relocated in 1891. In 2000 the world's largest *torii* gate was erected at the original site, marking the entrance to this perpetually sacred space.

Fox guardian statues are plentiful at Inari shrines. Their mouths may hold a key, a scroll, a ball or round jewel, or a rice stalk. These auspicious symbols represent access to the storehouse (bounty), messages from the gods, prosperity, and the harvest. Red is a protection color that wards off evil—hence, the reason red bibs can be found on statues representing various *kami* and Buddhist deities as well.

"Installation of the Sun Goddess" after a work by Kawanabe Kyosai. The divine parents Izanami and Izanagi stand at the right. The sun goddess Amaterasu, giver of light and warmth, is considered chief of the Shinto deities.

Omamori—talismans—are a fusion of Shinto and Buddhism. There are various types, and each type serves a specific purpose, such as to attract luck, ensure safety, assist in academic performance, and so on. The style pictured here houses a prayer inscribed on paper or wood. It is meant to be worn or carried for a year, after which time its power is depleted and it should be replaced with a fresh one.

Ema plaques are purchased, inscribed with the visitors' prayers, and hung in a designated spot at the shrine, where they'll remain for a certain amount of time, then be removed and ritually burned. If you look closely, you may be able to note that not all of the prayers pictured here are written in Japanese. This changes nothing—in Shinto, all are welcome.

Worms and creepy-crawlies in Studio Ghibli movies—not all bad guys are completely wicked

In the preceding myth we saw how Izanami is transformed into a shapeless mass covered in worms. This terrifying image associated with death is a recurring theme in Japanese art.

In Hayao Miyazaki's *Nausicaä of the Valley of the Wind*, humanity survives on a contaminated planet. Beside a desert, there is a forest where mutant creatures live—some of them, like the Ohm, are the size of a building. It is a toxic forest where humans need to wear masks to survive.

In the battles between humans and the toxic forest creatures (creepy-crawlies dreamed up by Hayao Miyazaki's imagination) appear, often looking and moving like Izanami's maggots and worms. Many people advocate the total destruction of the forest, but Princess Nausicaä does not believe the mutant creatures are evil.

Miyazaki's *Princess Mononoke* is set in the Muromachi Period and tells the story of the fight between a forest's spirit custodians and the humans desecrating its resources.

At the start of the movie, Prince Ashitaka fights a demon that is destroying his village. The demon is a shapeless black mass with strands that writhe like worms.

Ashitaka manages to kill it with an arrow, at which point the now dead "worms" disappear and are revealed to be covering the body of a wild boar. This is Nago, a boar *kami* that was possessed by evil spirits and changed into a *tatarigami* (祟り神: "possessed *kami*").

Ashitaka emerges victorious but is left with a wound on his arm, and through this wound a curse has been passed onto him. The village elders tell him that when he gives in to negative emotions like anger or hatred, his injured arm will be covered in black worms like the ones that completely enveloped the boar's body.

As well as the association of creepy-crawlies with corruption, in these two Miyazaki works another recurring theme is the belief that evil is not something absolute that belongs to something or someone forever. Judging someone too hastily can lead us to false conclusions. Good or evil can change.

This morality, in which things are not all black or white, but may have different shades of gray, is entrenched in Japanese culture. It is unusual to find Japanese novels or movies where the good guys and the bad guys destroy one another completely.

In *Dragon Ball*, by Akira Toriyama, even the most terrifying enemies, who in principle wanted to destroy planet Earth, end up becoming friends of the main character Son Goku. Even Piccolo (the Great Demon King) stops being evil and joins the good guys. And although the fearsome Vegeta—one of the most powerful beings in the universe—tries to wipe out humanity, in the end something in his heart changes and he marries Bulma, Son Goku's best friend.

A cultural reflection—the culture of shame

It is interesting that as far back as in one of Japan's oldest myths, shame should be present as a watershed moment. Izanami cannot bear the shame she feels when her husband sees what she has become after her death. Her horror at being seen in such a terrible state and the sting of betrayal are so strong that she refuses to return with him.

Ruth Benedict, in her book *The Chrysanthemum and the Sword*, described Japanese culture as "shame culture" and compared it to American culture, which she described as "guilt culture."

Ultimately, what motivates the actions of the Japanese (in general)? Not suffering shame, not suffering humiliation.

Oftentimes, when dealing with Japanese companies, or speaking to the Japanese, whether from overseas or in Japan, we will notice certain types of odd behavior that might surprise us. But if we consider that shame is one of the greatest motivators in this culture, perhaps we will acquire a better understanding of the situation.

Why is my friend Watanabe so reluctant to have her photo taken in public? Undoubtedly it is because she is ashamed to be seen by others while she is being photographed. She may not be alone in this, and it may be kindest to ask your subject if they'd prefer to be photographed in a secluded place.

Why doesn't a company from Nagoya want to sign a partnership contract that in other cultures would be considered a triviality? Probably not because of money-related issues, but because of the risk of things going badly and being discussed in the media, which would be an embarrassment for the company.

Amaterasu and Susanoo Are Born

When Izanagi returned from the netherworld, after his failed rescue mission, he had to submit to a purification ceremony.

During the ceremony, when he proceeded to wash his face, Amaterasu emerged from one of his eyes. She is the Sun *kami* and is considered to be the greatest of the *kami* and the mother of Japan. As Izanagi continued washing his face, Susanoo emerged from his nose; he is the god of the sea, storms and of war, a *kami* with a fickle personality.

There are dozens of stories about the quarrels between Amaterasu and Susanoo.

They decided to solve one of their arguments by trial (competition, *ukehi*) at which they would compete to see who could create the most divinities. Amaterasu declared herself the winner of the test because she had created several male *kami* using her necklace (*magatama*). Susanoo also produced several female deities and, angry at his sister's arrogant attitude, declared he was the true winner. As they couldn't come to an agreement, Susanoo was possessed by a fit of rage and destroyed his sister's rice fields.

He also decided to destroy the spinning mill where his sister was making a tunic to offer to the gods. Susanoo threw a "heavenly horse" (天の斑駒) that fell backwards into the room where the tunics were made and destroyed it. According to the *Kojiki*, one of the spinners (Wakahirume) was killed. The fall was so dreadful the horse also died.

Amaterasu grew so angry she hid herself in a cave (see Chapter 2—Shimenawa). When she shut herself away, the light disappeared from the universe.

Her brother Susanoo appeared before the council of the "eight hundred *kami*," who accused him of murdering the heavenly horse, killing the spinner Wakahirume and scaring his sister, thus plunging the universe into darkness. He was banished and sent to the Izumo region.

Up until this point, the legend depicts Susanoo as a malicious, provocative, arrogant and even evil creature. But, during his banishment his attitude changed. There he met a couple who were suffering because they had lost seven of their eight daughters—they had been devoured by a giant snake called Yamata no Orochi (八俣遠呂智). The eighth daughter, who was called Kushinadahime, was in danger—she was going to be the snake's next victim.

Susanoo decided to help. To stop the monster from finding her, he transformed Kushinadahime, the eighth daughter, into a comb, which he placed in his hair. He then persuaded the giant snake to drink *sake*. When he managed to get it drunk and it was sufficiently groggy, he took advantage of the chance to kill it.

From the tail of the snake's corpse, a sword appeared. Later, with the aim of patching things up with his sister and being forgiven for his misdeeds, Susanoo gave this sword to his sister Amaterasu.

The sword, called Kusanagi, is regarded as one of the three imperial treasures of Japan. The other two treasures are the Yata mirror and a jeweled Magatama necklace. These three objects are the property of the imperial household, and their location is unknown, although the sword is rumored to be in the Atsuta Shrine in Nagoya, the necklace in the Imperial Palace in Tokyo and the mirror in the Ise Shrine in Mie.

They represent three virtues:

- Valor (the Kusanagi sword).
- Wisdom (the Yata mirror).
- Benevolence (the Magatama necklace).

Amaterasu, who had received the sword as a gift from her brother, decided to give it to her grandson Ninigi, along with the mirror and the necklace. She then entrusted him with the mission of descending from the celestial plane in order to go and pacify Japan.

Ninigi took the three treasures with him, which would eventually end up in the hands of his great-grandson Jimmu, the first Emperor of Japan.

Jimmu, the First Emperor

Jimmu is considered to be the founder and first Emperor of Japan. Nearly all historians agree he is a legendary figure. There is no proof he existed, but there is a written record of his exploits in both the *Nihon Shoki* and the *Kojiki*.

Legend has it he ruled from the year 660 BCE until 585 BCE and was a direct descendant of the gods; Amaterasu, the Sun *kami*, had ordered her grandson Ninigi to descend from the celestial plane and journey to Earth.

Once he had settled down with humans, Ninigi married Konohana. They had three sons and both he and his children lost the power of immortality. Several generations later Jimmu was born.

If you follow the family tree closely, the goddess Amaterasu—the chief god of Japan—is Ninigi's grandmother, who in turn is Jimmu's great-grandmother. All the Emperors of Japan up until the present-day are descendants of Jimmu.

Although it is a myth, the literal interpretation of the divine lineage of the members of the imperial household was regarded as an absolute truth until the end of the Second World War. In early 1946, complying with the orders of general Douglas MacArthur, Emperor Hirohito officially announced: "The ties between Us and Our people have always stood on mutual trust and affection. They do not depend upon mere legends and myths. They are not predicated on the false conception that the Emperor is divine, and that the Japanese people are superior to other races and fated to rule the world."

Jimmu led a military expedition that ranged from the southwest to the north-east and eventually managed to conquer the Yamato region. A three-legged crow guided them during the expedition showing them the way to go. According to Chinese folklore, three-legged crows have lived in the Sun. This mythological crow is known in Japanese as *yatagarasu* and nearly always appears in paintings and works of art connected with the first Emperor.

Jimmu and his soldiers looking at the *yatagarasu* (three-legged crow) that guided their expedition in the military conquest of Yamato.

The logo of Japan's national soccer team is a three-legged crow.

The Zelda mythology

The creators of *Zelda* say that part of the inspiration for their games comes from their surroundings. The Nintendo offices are in Kyoto and its employees often visit shrines and temples in the city and its outskirts. Inevitably they end up including Shintoist (and also Buddhist) elements and mythology in their video games.

Part of the story of the *Legend of Zelda* video games franchise is inspired by Shinto. The *Legend of Zelda* world was created by three gods: Din created the mountains and the landscapes, Nayru the water and the sky, and Farore the trees and creatures of the world. When their work was done, they abandoned the world, but before doing so they left behind three golden triangles: the Triforce.

In this video game story, we can see certain similarities with the Japanese creation myth: in Japanese myth Amaterasu is the Sun goddess, Tsukuyomi is the moon deity, and Susanoo is the storm god. When they finished their labors of creation and returned to the heavenly plane, they left behind three imperial treasures in Japan. Maybe this is the inspiration for the video game's Triforce?

Other interesting points that are clearly inspired by Shinto:

- In the latest Zelda games for the Nintendo Switch console there are locations called shrines (*jinja* in the Japanese version) where you have to go to solve puzzles.
- The maps of castles and dungeons look like Shintoist shrine maps.
- The importance of the role of nature is another of the characteristics of Hyrule, the Zelda universe, which is inhabited by spirits that dwell in mountains, springs, lakes and forests.
- In the game *The Legend of Zelda: Ocarina of Time*, one of the lead character's mentors is the Great Deku—a talking tree. Its behavior is inspired by the *shinboku* (sacred trees) of Shinto.
- One of the most common Zelda game mechanics is to give the player a mission consisting of freeing a mountain, a lake, a tree, a village, a town or territory, a person or animal, etc. that has been contaminated by some evil entity. That is, as players we have to control Link, the protagonist, and go around "purifying" what has been contaminated. In Chapter 5, we shall look in more depth at the meaning of "purification" (*harai*) and "contamination" or "corruption" (*kegare*).
- One of the Zelda games' most important messages is similar to that found in Ghibli movies: modern society tends to abuse nature and it is important to remember we must live in harmony with it. Recovering humanity's connection with our surroundings is fundamental.

CHAPTER **4**

THE SHINTOIST SHRINE

ℬ • ℭ

"With sincerity, there is virtue."
– Japanese proverb of Shintoist origin

Shrine Structure

Although the structure of Shintoist shrines changes depending on the architectural style of each region, there are certain elements that tend to be repeated. Here are the most common ones:

1. *Torii*: shrine entrance.
2. Stairs: not all shrines have them, but they are a typical element when they are located on hillsides.
3. *Sandō:* main path.
4. *Temizu-ya* or *Chōzu-ya*: place for washing your hands and mouth. It is important to purify oneself before going on to visit the shrine.
5. *Tōrō:* stone lamps. They are usually unlit and are lit only for celebrations. They originate from China and the observant traveler will find them practically everywhere in Asia.
6. *Kagura-den*: stage where *kagura* dance and / or *Noh* theater performances are carried out.
7. *Shamusho*: shrine office where administrative tasks are carried out. Pursuant to a law from the year 1951, shrines are exempt from paying taxes, but they do have certain obligations when it comes to reporting their activities.
8. *Ema:* wooden plaques where visitors may write their wishes. The place assigned for hanging them usually has a small wooden roof to protect them from the rain.
9. *Sessha* or *setsumatsusha:* small ancillary shrines.
10. *Komainu or Inari* foxes: statues of guard dogs (*Komainu*) or *Inari* foxes. They are usually at both ends of the *sandō*.
11. *Haiden:* prayer hall open to the public.
12. *Tamagaki:* (normally wooden) fence enclosing the *honden*.
13. *Honden:* building that houses the shrine's main *kami*.

Types of Shrines

Although not all shrines may be classified, most of them fall into the following categories:

Imperial Shrines

These shrines were founded and administered by the government during the period of State Shinto (国家神道: *Kokka shinto*) that ended in 1945. Some of Japan's most important shrines fall into this category, and the most visited are: the Ise shrine in Mie (Ise Jingū), the Izumo shrine in Shimane (Izumo Taisha), the Meiji shrine in Tokyo (Meiji Jingū) and the Heian shrine in Kyoto (Heian Jingū).

You can easily recognize imperial shrines if you pay attention to the following:

The Japanese term to refer to shrines is normally *jinja* 神社, but in the case of imperial shrines the word *jingū* 神宮 is used.

The imperial emblem of Japan, in the guise of a chrysanthemum flower, is usually visible at the entrance and also in subtle features found inside the shrine grounds.

A lamp featuring the imperial emblem of Japan.

Inari Shrines

Inari shrines are devoted to Inari, the *kami* of fertility and rice. This is the most numerous type—there are over 30,000, and the Fushimi Inari in Kyoto is one of the most famous and most visited in the country. They are easily recognized thanks to the presence of fox statues, normally at the entrance. The fox is regarded as one of Inari's messengers.

Hachiman Shrines

Hachiman shrines are devoted to Hachiman, the *kami* of war. This is the second most numerous type after the Inari class. One of the most visited in Japan is the Tsurugaoka Hachimangu shrine in Kamakura, and the most important is the Usa-Jingū in the Oita prefecture.

You can easily recognize Hachiman shrines if you pay attention to the following:

- Instead of fox statues, they are usually guarded by two *komainu* statues (lion dogs).
- Part of the *haiden* roof is curved.
- The *torii* gates have two upper lintels and the ends of them slope down slightly.

Tenjin Shrines

Tenjin shrines are devoted to the *kami* of Sugawara Michizane, a scholar and politician from the Heian Period. They are specially popular among students preparing for their entrance examinations. Tenjin shrines may be recognized by their ox statues and plum trees—Michizane's favorite tree. The most famous Tenjin shrine is Dazaifu Tenmangu, near Fukuoka.

Asama or Sengen Shrines

Asama or Sengen shrines (浅間神社) are devoted to Princess Konohanasakuya-hime, the *kami* of Mount Fuji and also of other volcanoes in Japan. There are more than a thousand shrines devoted to her, but the most important ones are located in the foothills and at the summit of Mount Fuji. Most of them have views of Mount Fuji or other volcanoes.

Popular belief has it that worshipping Princess Konohanasakuya-hime prevents Mount Fuji from erupting. Even so, there are historical records of eighteen eruptions on Mount Fuji and we also know that some volcanic eruptions in Kyūshū destroyed shrines devoted to her.

Sanshiro Sugata—**Akira Kurosawa**

In Akira Kurosawa's movie *Sanshiro Sugata*, the lead character refers to the importance of Japan's most famous volcano and credits the *kami* with its creation:

"The spirits of heaven and earth congregate in our nation of gods. For us they have built Mt. Fuji that towers for eternity. For us they have brought water to flow around our islands. For us they have created the beauty of cherry blossoms."

Sanshiro Sugata is a young man who is accepted into the judo school run by master Shogoro Yano. From the first day, master Yano realizes Sanshiro is physically superior to the other students but lacks self-control and discipline.

After seeing Sanshiro get into a street fight at a village festival, master Yano gets angry and tells him that if he has such little mental discipline, to carry on teaching him judo would be like giving a madman a knife. Shocked by his master's words, Sanshiro leaps into a slimy mud-filled pond to demonstrate his strength and loyalty.

Clinging on to a post in the pond, he stays afloat for a day and a night. When he is about to sink from exhaustion and drown in the mud, he sees a lotus flower bud open (he also hears the opening—the lotus flower generates a characteristic sound when it opens). This is the moment when he realizes his master was right, gets out of the pond and runs to ask Yano for forgiveness and tell him that he now understands there is more to life than just muscle and fighting.

Sanshiro Sugata observing the lotus flower. This is the movie's key moment, when he realizes he has to change his attitude regarding the aim and worth of martial arts.

This scene is a visual representation of the word *deichunohasu*, 泥中之蓮: でいちゅうのはす which means "From out of the mud and dirt the lotus blooms." In other words, without the mud the lotus cannot bloom.

Metaphorically it also means that someone who is deeply flawed or is going through a hard time can see difficulties as a muddy pond where flowers will bloom in the future.

The mud symbolizes life's adversities, challenges and difficulties, while the lotus represents the growth, purity and beauty that stem from these difficult circumstances.

Other Types of Shrines

Apart from the most common styles, there are also shrines devoted to local *kami* and ones that were built to honor powerful leaders and families. The best-known example is Nikko (to the north of Tokyo), where on a lush forest-covered mountain slope, dozens of shrines were built devoted to—among others—Tokugawa Ieyasu (the first shogun of the Edo Period).

Nikko was one of the first places I visited when I arrived in Japan. I still have very vivid memories of the fascination it made me feel inside. I recall walking in the woods at dawn, the fog still thick on the ground, and suddenly seeing the silhouette of a pagoda emerging from among the trees. I was amazed by the amount of moss-covered stone *tourou* lanterns, the *torii* gates (and also Chinese style *mon* gates), the mixture of architectural styles, the gaze of the protective *nioh*…

Although I didn't understand anything at all—I didn't even know what a *torii* gate was—I could feel it was a special place. Nikko transported me to another dimension.

Later, after visiting the place several times, I learned that the complex made up of the Futara-san, and Tōshō-gū shrines and the Rinnō-ji temple are a crystal-clear example of syncretism: a mixture of Buddhist and Shintoist styles and beliefs.

The Nikko complex shrines (Futara-san and Tōshō-gū shrines and Rinnō-ji temple) are recognized as a World Heritage Site.

Shintoist Architecture

The architecture of Shintoist shrines can be sorted into many styles: *Taisha-zukuri, Sumiyoshi-zukuri* and *Shinmei-zukuri, Hagare-zukuri, Hachiman-zukuri, Kazuga-zukuri, Otori-zukuri…*

Here I will focus on explaining two of the most ancient styles—*Shinmei-zukuri* and *Taisha-zukuri*—which laid down their founding principles before the arrival of Buddhism. Then, I shall describe the characteristics of *Nagare-zukuri,* which borrowed elements from Buddhism and imported ideas from Chinese architecture.

Shinmei-zukuri

This style evolved naturally from the construction methods of houses and barns where rice was stored during the Yayoi and Kofun periods (from the third century BCE up until the sixth century CE). Simplicity is its distinguishing feature: the use of untreated wood, raised floors, low-rise buildings, cylindrical columns, straight lines and straw triangular-shaped roofs.

The Nishina Shinmei (Nagano) and Ise Jingū (Mie) shrines are the most important examples of this style still preserved today; the three of them were built for the first time before the seventh century. No one knows the exact date they were first established; some historians argue they are over two thousand years old, but we only know for sure that they appear in documents written in the seventh century.

Following the tradition established by the *shikinen-sengu* (式年遷宮) festivals, many shrines are rebuilt every so often. Normally every twenty years, but there are also cases where it is carried out every sixty or seventy years or more.

In the periodic reconstructions they use the original maps, the same materials (wood from the forest and straw from indigenous grasses for the roofs), ancient tools (the use of cranes, chainsaws or electrical tools is not permitted) and the original methods (the use of metal nails is not permitted).

In other cultures, the conservation of original buildings and objects is valued; there is an attempt to alter as little as possible and only that which is strictly necessary is restored, even if that results in the building's appearance declining with the passing of time. In the case of Shintoist architecture, and we could also say of Japanese culture in general, the emphasis tends to be placed on the traditions, methods and ways of constructing or creating a work of art.

The Japanese Zen Buddhist proverb *shogyomujou* (諸行無常) literally means "nothing endures," that is, nothing lasts forever nor does it remain always in the same form or state. Accepting the universe's transitory nature is one of the fundamental principles of Buddhism, but it is not easy, since we humans tend toward the contrary—to want or wish for nothing to change. We find it hard to face our mortality and the finite nature of our planet and universe.

The Second Law of Thermodynamics works against humanity. What is the best option—to allow buildings to get old with the passing of time or to rebuild them every so often? Or to renovate only when necessary altering original structures as little as possible?

The answers to these metaphysical questions have been debated not only in Japan but in the whole world for thousands of years. Heraclitus said it with his famous "No man ever steps in the same river twice. For it's not the same river and he's not the same man." As did Plutarch when he explained the Theseus paradox:

> *"The ship wherein Theseus and the youth of Athens returned from Crete had thirty oars, and was preserved by the Athenians down even to the time of Demetrius Phalereus, for they took away the old planks as they decayed, putting in new and stronger timber in their places, insomuch that this ship became a standing example among the philosophers, for the logical question of things that grow; one side holding that the ship remained the same, and the other contending that it was not the same."*
>
> – Plutarch, Life of Theseus 23.1

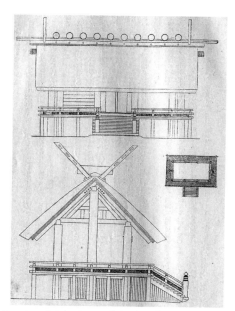

Front and side views of the *honden* at Ise Jingū.

A photograph I took in the year 2011 at a now disappeared Ise Jingū. In 2013 a new reconstruction was inaugurated that will remain standing until 2033.

Taisha-zukuri

Izumo Taisha, in the Shimane prefecture, is one of the most important exponents of *taisha-zukuri* architecture.

No one knows exactly when Izumo Taisha was established (in modern-day Shimane prefecture), but many historians regard it as one of the oldest shrines in Japan. There is a written record as far back as the eighth century describing its *honden* as one of the most majestic wooden buildings in Japan.

The size of its buildings contrasts with those of Ise Jingū. While the *shinmei-zukuri* style of Ise Jingū is subtle and gives the impression that the aim is to integrate with the forest surroundings, in the case of Izumo Taisha the style is more imposing.

The double-sided roofs and the gable ends are majestic—they rise to a height of 24 meters (80 feet). The flooring is raised quite some way above the forest floor, something that was common in barns back in ancient times (to keep vermin out).

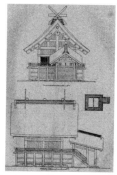

In these front and side views of Izumo Taisha we can appreciate its considerable height above the ground and the roof's great size.

The *taisha-zukuri* architecture of Izumo Taisha in the Shimane prefecture is characterized by buildings that are somewhat higher than those that follow the precepts of *shinmei-zukuri* architecture. There is also a little more separation between the surrounding forest and the sacred grounds marked out by the *tamagaki* (wooden fence).

Isometric map that was attached to the proposal sent to the Emperor for the periodic reconstruction of Izumo Taisha in the year 1875.

Nagare-zukuri

This is the most widespread style. Its defining characteristics gradually developed once Buddhism spread across Japanese territory. It has a marked amount of asymmetry and curved lines in the roofs. *Nagare* means "flow" and is normally used to refer to a river current or water in a canal or pipe. *Zukuri* means "construction." The overall meaning could be interpreted as "construction that flows," alluding to the curved roofs that look like ocean waves.

Normally the main *honden* entrance is not in the frontage but at one of the sides. This type of entrance is known as *hirairi* (平入).

The Ujigami shrine in Uji (Kyoto prefecture); we can discern the curved roofs typical of *nagare-zukuri*.

"To be fully alive is to have an aesthetic perception of life because a major part of the world's goodness lies in its often unspeakable beauty."

— Yukitaka Yamamoto

CHAPTER 5

RITUALS, FESTIVALS AND CEREMONIES

৪০ • ০৪

"Rituals are the music of life."
– Nassim Taleb

Ritualism

The first time I attended a tea ceremony I was expecting to enjoy the drink and to chat with my friends. But when the day came, I recall not being able to bear the strong, bitter taste of the *matcha*. We spent so long sitting on the *tatami* listening to the master of ceremonies' instructions—how to sit correctly, how to hold the bowl before bringing it to your lips, etc.—that I ended up tired and with aching legs. I recall that my opinion and that of European colleagues who attended the ceremony with me was something along the lines of: "The tea was undrinkable and we've spent more time learning the right way to hold a bowl than chatting. What a letdown!" We were young and maybe at the time our minds were not sufficiently open to understanding experiences that were different to the ones we had been used to since childhood.

In time I came to understand that the purpose of the tea ceremony is not to chat with friends like you do in a street cafe on the shore of the Mediterranean.

Japanese culture is very sensitive to the "context." That is to say, we have to change and adapt our behavior to the situation we are in, understanding that there are a series of implicit social norms or rules that are not apparent at first sight. In my book *The Magic of Japan* (Tuttle Publishing) I explained in detail the importance of non-verbal communication and how "high context" leads to Japanese society being considered collectivist.

Now I drink *matcha* almost every day, use a traditional bowl and a whisk (*chasen*) made out of bamboo wood to get just the amount of froth I like. I love the bitter taste and have learned to enjoy each step of the process. When I have the chance to attend a tea ceremony (*chadō*), I appreciate the feeling of being transported to a parallel world. I revel in the peace and quiet it imbues me with. Different contexts lead us to feeling and acting differently.

At the age of twenty-three, I didn't understand anything—I didn't know to "read the context." Now that I am nearly twice as old, I understand that even though the tea is at the center of the ceremony, whether or not you like the taste is irrelevant. The most important thing is to take part in the ritual.

The key to a ritual is to follow the steps. "Just do it!" The first karate lesson Mr. Miyagi gives in the movie *Karate Kid* is based on this principle. Mr. Miyagi instructs Daniel to clean his cars following two steps: "Wax on, wax off." In martial arts, repetition of the simplest movements or *kata* over many years is one of the keys to becoming a great master.

In modern terms, we talk about "habits" or "routines" to refer to actions we carry out automatically or almost unthinkingly. In reality, this is another way to talk about "rituals."

By nature, we humans are ritualistic creatures.

Dances, different ways of praying, the celebration of rites of passage, funerals and festivals have been factors common to any human settlement for thousands of years.

Before the birth of verbal communication and writing, knowledge and culture were transmitted from generation to generation through rituals. Our biology is designed to learn and feel whatever we do repeatedly.

Repetition is the mother of teaching.

Japanese education is criticized for putting too much emphasis on repetition and forgetting about critical thinking or creativity. But it turns out some of the most creative and original artists in the world are Japanese. Why?

"Shinto is something you do, rather than something you are."
— David Chart[12]

The Four Elements of Worship

According to Dr. Sokyo Ono (former professor at Kokugakuin University and speaker for Japan's Association of Shinto Shrines), all Shinto ceremonies and rites may be classified into one of these four elements[13]:

1. Purification (*Harai*).
2. Offering (*Shinsen*).
3. Prayer (*Norito*).
4. Symbolic feast (*Naorai*).

When an individual makes a private visit to a shrine, at least one of these elements is included.

Purification—Harai

Harai also known as *Ō-Harai*, is one of the fundamental ideas of Shinto. One of the interpretations of the word's origin is that it comes from *haraeau*, a combination of:

- *Hare* 晴: clear, clarity, clean, pure.
- *Au* 合: mutual, unite, unify.

By combining the two meanings we get: "clean or purify each other."[14] It can be interpreted both literally, in the sense that we

---

[12] From *Shinto Practice for Non-Japanese* by David Chart, Independently published in 2020.

[13] From *Shinto: the Kami Spirit World of Japan* by Soyo Ono, 2nd ed. Tuttle Publishing, 2024.

[14] As intepreted by Motohisa Yamakage in *The Essence of Shinto: Japan's Spiritial Heart*, Kodansha International, 2012.

are dirty, or also metaphorically referring to the morality of our actions. That is, if we have acted wrongly, if we have "sinned" or made mistakes, we are "dirty." In Japanese, instead of "sin," they use the words *tsumi* (罪: violation of rules) or *kegare* (穢れ・汚れ: dishonor, defilement, corruption).

The difference with other religions in which we must confess our sins in order to be forgiven, is that in Shinto there is no confession, nor are we forgiven—we are simply "cleaned." Another peculiarity is that there is also the possibility that the *kami* are the ones who are "corrupt" and it is partly our responsibility to free the *kami* from their "dirtiness" or "wickedness."

One of the easiest ways to purify yourself is to rinse out your mouth and wash your hands in a *temizu-ya* (see Chapter 2) at the entrance to a shrine. In more formal purification ceremonies, a *kannushi* (priest) also intervenes by praying for us and waving a rod (or *sakaki* branch, depending on the shrine) above our heads. Depending on the type of ceremony, those present are also sprinkled with saltwater. The act of purifying with water is called *misogi*. Purification can be carried out not only on human beings but also on animals, objects and even buildings.

The possibility of something or someone being "dirty" is a recurring theme in Japanese literature, cinema, folk tales, anime and manga.

In *Dragon Ball*, only Son Goku's pure heart may climb aboard the *kinton* cloud. Even the supposedly good characters, Son Goku's comrades in arms, may not use the flying cloud since none of them has a heart that is 100% free of "dirtiness."

When the main character faces enemies, instead of killing them or completely eliminating them, he fights with them until he manages to "transform" them and they end up forming part of the good guys team. Even Piccolo, one of the most powerful enemies, and considered to be an embodiment of Satan, is freed from the "corruption that contaminates his being" (using literally translated Shinto terminology).

Evil is something that makes us suffer; if we detect it, our mission is to help. We humans are all in danger of being "contaminated."

There are many exceptions, but I cannot help but make the following generalizations:

- Western stories: good and evil are absolute. This evil is normally completely destroyed. The battle takes place between good and evil; only one side may win. Best-known example: *The Lord of the Rings*.
- Japanese stories: good and evil may flow or change. Enemies are purified or freed from the evil living inside them. Best-known example: *Dragon Ball*.

Harai in the movie *Spirited Away*

In the movie *Spirited Away* (千と千尋の神隠し *Sen to Chihiro no Kamikakushi*) directed by Hayao Miyazaki, the lead character Chihiro travels with her parents to a fantasy world. In the beginning, Chihiro's parents succumb to gluttony and are transformed into pigs.

To rescue her parents, Chihiro starts to work in an *onsen* (bathhouse) where the customers are *kami* who have been possessed by "dirtiness" and "corruption." One of the deities Chihiro has to serve bathes in the thermal springs and starts to vomit an enormous amount of junk. He turns out to be a river spirit, and the trash he throws up is a metaphor for the damage humans do when we pollute.

Kaonashi (No-Face), another of the bathhouse's customers, who slips into the complex without permission and can't stop guzzling down gold nuggets, represents greed. Even when Kaonashi transforms into a terrifying monster, Chihiro is brave enough to try to help him.

With her good heart, Chihiro cleans the evil that has possessed the gods and manages to "cure" even the most corrupt of them. At the end of the movie, even the wicked witch Yubaba ends up being good and we feel compassion for her.

Offering—Shinsen

Shinsen (神饌) offerings to the *kami* are normally one of three types:

- Money.
- Food or drink.
- Animals or material objects with a symbolic meaning.

Money is the most common offering. Shrines usually have an offerings box with a slot on the top that is meant for collecting coins. You should put coins in the box before making a wish or praying. If there is no box, there is usually a saucer with a pile of coins.

The tradition of offering the gods food, carefully placed on trays or plates, seems to be a factor common to many places in Asia regardless of the religion. It is something I have observed not only in Japan, but also in China, Korea, Thailand…

But the presentation and the food of the offerings can be extremely varied, and changes from one region or people to another. If it is an important shrine, there is usually a specific instructions manual: how to place the plates and trays, the type of food, which room you should carry out the preparation in, where to place the offerings, etc.

Typical offerings in Japan tend to be: rice, salt, water, *sake*, oranges, local fruit, vegetables, flowers, *sakaki* branches or leaves.

My mother-in-law, who lives in Okinawa, has a manual of over three hundred pages with diagrams and summaries detailing how to carry out offerings according to the tradition of the southern islands. Although she already knows it almost by heart (because she changes the offerings at the family altar every day) when the season changes or when there is some special celebration, I see how she consults the manual and makes small adjustments to the layout of the plates and food she offers.

Another option is to offer animals or material objects. Companies, associations, or rich families donate statues, *torii* gates, items of clothing (made of silk), and jewels. In ancient times, they also used to donate horses and chickens, but this is hardly ever seen nowadays, although the imperial family still donates white horses to the Ise shrine.

Prayer—Norito

Norito (liturgical texts) are recited in classical Japanese, which is hard to understand; even if you know modern Japanese, you need to study in order to understand it.

For my wedding ceremony, I had to memorize a two-page text. I began reciting it without knowing what I was saying, but after asking a lot of questions and using specific dictionaries, I understood it was a direct plea to the *kami* to unite my wife and I and to keep us healthy. It was also expressing gratitude and respect.

When the time came, my wife and I read out the text facing the empty courtyard at the center of the shrine.

That was the only moment when we had to speak. During the rest of the ceremony the other *norito* were read by the monks.

The Association of Shinto Shrines can provide prayers that may be freely used by everyone. But each shrine or person is free to modify them or create their own *norito* if they so desire.

Symbolic Feast—Naorai

Naorai, means "to eat or drink with the *kami*." This is a feast at which those attending a festivity conclude the celebration by eating what was first offered to the gods.

A simpler kind of *naorai* (without food) consists of drinking a little *sake* served on small plates by *miko* (shrine maidens) or *kannushi* (male monks). This act of drinking *sake* with the *kami* is performed at nearly all formal ceremonies: at *kekkonshiki* (weddings), *hatsumode* (first visit of the year), *jichinsai* (groundbreaking ceremony).

Feasts are also held on other important occasions.

Matsuri

The word *matsuri* (祭り) is usually translated as "festival," but its literal meaning is "to invite the *kami* to come or descend." The *kami* are believed to visit settlements and shrines every so often and you need to be ready in order to welcome them in the appropriate way.

Matsuri are celebrated all year round, although they are more common in the summer and on days when there is a change of season. In the winter *matsuri* people ask for life to return to the fields; in spring, they pray for a good harvest; in summer, people usually ask for protection against natural disasters; fall is the time when thanks are given for harvests.

Different regions celebrate them in different ways, but they often include music, dancing, theater, fair stalls and street food.

Most *matsuri* are divided into three parts, which can last for hours or days.

1. *Kamimukaesai* (神迎祭): this is the "greeting to welcome the *kami*" in the shrine. In this phase, the *kami* are invited to "descend" and take up temporary residence in a *shintai* object.
2. *Shinkōsai* (神幸祭): this is the "procession of the *kami*." The object where the *kami* is residing—the *shintai*—is placed inside a *mikoshi*. *Mikoshi* are miniature shrines made of wood. The act of parading the *mikoshi* through the streets is a symbolic gesture in which the main *kami* (temporarily residing in the *shintai*) is carried through the streets adjoining the shrine. My friend Sato has been taking part in the Kanda festival for a long time, and when the time comes for him to hoist a *mikoshi* on his shoulders, it is treated as an important topic of conversation. Carrying a *mikoshi* is normally a question of pride.
3. *Kami Okuri* (神送り): this is the ritual of "sending the *kami* back." Just as it is good manners to accompany a guest to the door when they leave, so it is important to guide the *kami* respectfully back home.

Mikoshi carried aloft in the *Sanja matsuri*, one of Tokyo's most important Shinto festivals.

A stripped down explanation: a *matsuri* consists of taking the *kami* out for a walk so they can be worshipped by everyone. Oddly enough, if we look at it like that, the parades in other parts of the world also follow the same general structure. For example, in Spain's Easter parades, the figure of the Virgin Mary is taken out of churches in towns and villages across the country and carried around the streets.

The most important celebrations that are common to all parts of Japan are: New Year (*hatsumode*), baptisms (*miyamairi*), weddings (*kekkonshiki*), coming of age day (*seijin-no-hi*), which is the second Monday in January for those reaching 20 years of age and the rite of passage for girls aged 3 and 7 and boys aged 3 and 5 (*shichi-go-san*).

Paprika

Paprika is the title of a 2006 movie directed by Satoshi Kon. One of the main themes is a downtown parade: it is a metaphor representing the subconscious and the repressed dreams present in many people's minds. The participants in this psychedelic parade carry *mikoshi* and all kinds of objects: statues, *torii* gates, *maneki nekos, darumas,* robots...

Satoshi Kon was inspired by Japanese *matsuri* but most of the elements are pure imagination. The Paprika festival is a metaphor for the chaos in the human subconscious. Strangely enough, many of the elements that appear can be related to desires and emotions: prosperity, good fortune, money, worries, fear, envy, jealousy...

List of the most popular *matsuri*

Listing all the *matsuri* that are celebrated each year would require an entire book—thousands are celebrated annually. Here are some of the best-known:

- Kanda (Tokyo): this is one of Tokyo's most important Shinto festivals.
- Sanja (Tokyo): this pays homage to the three men who founded Sensō-ji–Hinokuma Hamanari, Hinokuma Takenari and Hajino Nakatomo.
- Aomori Nebuta (Aomori): this is celebrated in late August in Aomori and is one of the most popular festivals with tourists.
- Gion matsuri (Kyoto): as well as *mikoshi* carried on people's shoulders, this *matsuri* features floats that can be over ten meters (33 feet) high taking to the streets.
- Kanamara (Kawasaki): is one of the most astonishing celebrations I have ever attended. It is devoted to fertility and the *mikoshi* are in the shape of large phalluses. Seeing the gigantic penises bobbing along the

streets of Kawasaki is surreal. It normally takes place on the first weekend of April.

- Nagasaki Kunchi (Nagasaki): is the most famous festival in Nagasaki. It began as a celebration of the fall harvests at the end of the sixteenth century and became a shrine festival when the Suwa Shrine was founded in 1614. Nagasaki Kunchi is the fall festival of Nagasaki's Suwa Shrine guardian deity and is celebrated every year across the whole city for three days from 7 October.

Hatsumode

I confess that one of my first cultural shocks was discovering how different New Year is here in Japan. In comparison with my experience in Spain, the Japanese New Year celebrations seemed extremely subdued to me. Over time I have got used to it and now appreciate both styles. In Japan, more emphasis is placed on celebrating New Year's Day than New Year's Eve.

Hatsumode (初詣) means "to make the first visit of the year to a shrine."

At my first *hatsumode*, I was surprised by the crowds of people at the Meiji Jingū Shrine. However, everyone stood in line in an orderly fashion waiting their turn.

When it was my turn, I copied what the others did: I deposited coins in the *saisenbako* (wooden donations box), bowed twice then clapped my hands twice, pressed my hands together with my eyes closed and expressed my gratitude for the good that had happened the previous year, and asked for protection and good luck for the year that had just begun. To finish, I clapped my hands a final time before leaving and making way for the next person.

That is the simplest way to celebrate *hatsumode*. It is a very personal thing—you simply visit the shrine to offer a few coins, express your gratitude and make a wish.

Years later, I had the chance to attend a more formal ceremony. After drinking a little *sake* from a saucer, we sat down on a *tatami* and a monk gave us a short talk. Part of the talk consisted of reading out the names of all the attendees and he then asked the *kami* for the new year to bring us good fortune. Next, we looked down at the ground and the monk shook a *sakaki* branch over our heads.

Crowds awaiting their turn to celebrate the *hatsumode*; on the bottom left, you can make out the *saisenbako*, wooden boxes where coins are offered before praying.

Saisen and Saisenbako

Saisen (賽銭) means "monetary offering to the *kami*, or *bodhisattvas*." It is the generic term used both in Shinto shrines and Buddhist temples.

Saisenbako (賽銭箱) is the box used for collecting the coins. It is usually made of wood and is designed to make it easy to drop coins into it. It is rude to throw coins at it.

Five-yen coins are one of the most popular offerings because the Japanese for "five Yen" (五円) is pronounced "go-en," and means "harmonious relationship or union between people" (御縁).

Misogi

Misogi is a term that encompasses purification rituals (*harai*) in which water plays a central role. Water has a twin symbology: purification and connection to nature.

The traditional *misogi* is performed by bathing in waterfalls, the sea, rivers or lakes.

When I attended a *misogi* at a waterfall in the mountains to the east of Kanto, the men were dressed in *fundoshi* (traditional underwear) and the women wore a white kimono. Once we were almost naked, the ceremony leader took us from the shrine to the waterfall. There we recited several *norito*, then he went on to show us a series of warm-up exercises. He made us shake our hands up and down, move our legs backwards and forwards, clench our fists, etc. We also did an exercise called *torifune* (bird boat) in which we imitated a rowing motion while singing a series of "*Kotodama*': *ei ie!, ei ho!, ei sa!*" It is believed that the pronunciation of certain sounds has the power to change our mental state.

This exercise is also called *funa kogi no undo* (舟漕ぎの運動: rowing boat exercise) and is known to those who practice aikido. Morihei Ueshiba, the founder of this martial art, practiced *misogi* assiduously in the Nachi waterfalls. He placed a lot of value on spiritual purification and the "body-mind harmony." He came to the conclusion that "aikido is *misogi*." Having finished the exercises, we took turns throwing a handful of salt into the waterfall. Then we stepped below the torrent of water allowing it to pummel our back, neck and head.

Despite the warm-up exercises, what I most remember about the experience is the shock when I felt the jolt of cold water on the back of my neck.

Jichinsai

Jichinsai is the groundbreaking ceremony that takes place on a building site before beginning a new construction. The aim is to purify (*harai*) the site and ask the *kami* for everything to go well with the future house or building. Celebrating *jichinsai* is commonplace both for private houses and for commercial buildings or government constructions.

When Elon Musk visited Japan for the first time to set up Tesla, the headline photos showed the CEO bowing to a *kannushi* (monk) next to a pile of sand and, later, striking the pile of sand with a mallet—this was the *jichinsai* ceremony before the construction of Tesla's first building in Japan.

At one of the *jichinsai* I have attended, I had the honor of being one of the people who breaks down the "sand mountain" at the end of the ceremony. The chairman of the building company gave me a wooden mallet and when the *kannushi* gave me the order, I hit the top of the cone-shaped pile of sand. The chairman gave it a second blow, which knocked it down completely. All those attending applauded. Our little contribution officially marked the end of the *jichinsai* and the beginning of the construction.

Prior to getting our round of applause, we had witnessed each one of the steps in the *jichinsai* ceremony, led by the *kannushi*:

1. He purified (*harai* or *harae*) the altar and the attendees using an *oonusa*—a wooden rod adorned with pieces of paper.
2. The *kannushi* attracted the attention of the *kami* so they would heed our call and left offerings at the altar.
3. The *kannushi* recited a *norito* to bless the land. He also recited the names of the architect, constructor, developer etc. and requested good fortune for them and their families.
4. Next, the *kannushi* blessed each of the four corners of the site using salt and rice. Normally, before the ceremony, a square is marked out with poles and ropes; if the site is very big, only a small patch is covered. It reminded me of a *himorogi* (see Chapter 1).
5. *Jichin no gi* (地鎮の儀): this is the best part. The landowners, the developer, architect and/or builder strike a pile of sand with a wooden mallet (a shovel or hoe can also be used).
6. The attendees were given a *tamagushi* (*sakkaki* branch adorned with *washi* paper folded in the shape of *shide*), which was placed in the altar as an offering.
7. Finally, we drank *sake* from saucers.

Kagura, the Dance of the Gods

The first time I saw a *kagura* performance in Nagano, I felt like I had been transported to another time and place. The dancers moved with such subtlety they seemed to float above the *tatami*. Their gazes were fixed on Nagano's mountainous horizon. Their hands waved *kagura suzu* (wooden wands with bells) as they danced to the rhythm of the flute players' music. When they moved their arms, the long sleeves of their dresses rippled, achieving an almost hypnotic effect on those of us in the audience. The appearance of the *kagura suzu* reminded me of the hyssop Catholic priests use to sprinkle holy water.

The *kagura* (神: *kami*, 楽: to have fun) is a Shinto ceremonial dance. Etymologically speaking, it comes from the contraction of *kamukura kamikura* (神座), which means "place where the *kami* sit" or "place that the *kami* descend to."

It may be interpreted as a celebration in which we humans dance with the *kami* to entertain them.

I recommend the movie *Kagura me* (2015) directed by Yasuo Okuaki. It is the story of a girl and her father, who drift apart after the death of the mother, and reconcile through the practice of the *kagura* dance.

Kagura dancer, work by Suzuki Haranobu (1725–1770).

CHAPTER **6**

BUDDHISM, CONFUCIANISM
AND TAOISM

ℰℴ • ℭ℟

"The master ceases to be so when he loses the beginner's spirit."
– Japanese proverb

The Three Vinegar Tasters

The three vinegar tasters is an allegorical image that shows three old men trying vinegar. The painting symbolically embodies each one of the fundamental teachings of Confucianism, Buddhism and Taoism.

Rendering of the three vinegar tasters painted by an artist from the Kanō school (sixteenth century).

The cauldron filled with vinegar symbolizes the "essence of life" and the three men represent Confucianism, Buddhism and Taoism. The differences between each of the philosophies are expressed through their facial reactions to the vinegar's taste:

1. **Confucianism:** the Confucian character, often identified as Confucius himself, reacts with a sour expression. Confucianism considers life to be bitter since we have to have rules and laws in order to control the "moral degeneration inherent to the nature of human beings." It is important to maintain social harmony following strict ethical behavior in keeping with the established rules.

2. **Buddhism:** the Buddhist character, commonly associated with Gautama Buddha, has a bitter expression. This bitterness represents suffering as a fundamental aspect of human existence. Fighting against this reality generates more suffering, therefore, Buddhism holds that the best strategy when things do not go well is "acceptance." Vinegar is bitter, so to react with a bitter expression is to accept the reality of vinegar's nature just as it is.

3. **Taoism:** the Taoist character, which represents the teachings of Lao Tzu, has a smiling face. This happy reaction symbolizes the Taoist philosophy of gracefully embracing the natural flow of life. Whatever happens, whether life blows hot or cold, be flexible in order to face everything with a smile. Taoism considers life to be sweet since fundamentally everything is "perfect" in its natural state.

"From the Taoist point of view, sourness and bitterness come from the interfering and unappreciative mind. Life itself, when understood and utilized for what it is, is sweet. That is the message of 'The Vinegar Tasters.'"

– Benjamin Hoff, *The Tao of Pooh*

The harmonious coexistence of these three philosophies is described by the Chinese word *sanjiao* ("three teachings"). One of the first references to this idea of a three-way life union is attributed to Li Shiqian, a sixth-century scholar, who wrote: "Buddhism is the sun, Taoism the moon and Confucianism the five planets."[15] This tells us that although they are independent religions, they need one another just as the heavenly bodies are all important in order for the solar system to work.

Another popular proverb goes: "The three teachings—Taoism's gold and cinnabar, the relics of the Buddhist figures, and the Confucian virtues of humanity and integrity—are a tradition."

Syncretism

Syncretism is the mixture of different practices, symbols and religious beliefs. Buddhism was introduced to Japan between the third and sixth centuries, and a large part of it was integrated into the then emerging Shinto. They lived side by side for centuries to the point that the dividing line between the two traditions was hard to distinguish. At the same time, both Buddhism and Shinto were influenced by a melting pot of ideas and rules from Confucianism and Taoism.

During the Meiji Restoration in the year 1868, one of the great changes introduced to the country was the separation of Buddhism and Shinto via a process called *shinbutsu-bunri* (神仏分離: *kami*, *hotoke* or Buddhas, separation) through which classificatory bases were laid down to differentiate between the Shintoist *kami* and a *hotoke* or Buddha from Buddhism. Since then, Buddhism and Shinto have been considered independent traditions.

---

[15] This translation of Li Yanshou's observation can be found in *Beishi*. Bona ed. (Beijing: *Zhonghua shuju*, 1974), p. 1234. Translation from Chinese by Stephen F. Teiser. For more see the AFE: The Chinese Cosmos article "Sanjiao: the Three Teachings." http://afe.easia.columbia.edu/cosmos/ort/teachings.htm

Buddhism

One of the fundamental principles of Buddhism is that as a consequence of our existence, we human beings have to deal with *dukkha*: suffering or dissatisfaction. This refers not only to physical suffering but also to psychological suffering, however subtle it might be. Something as simple as wanting to buy a new couch, not being satisfied with a restaurant meal or wanting more attention from your spouse, are all examples of situations in which we feel *dukkha*.

The less we wish for, the happier we are.

Accepting the fleeting nature (諸行無常: *shogyomujou*) of everything that exists is another Buddhist tenet. Creatures live and die, and material objects change or disappear; nothing exists forever. The universe's only constant is change. Even so, we humans tend to worry excessively about the past and the future, instead of concentrating on the beauty of each moment in the present.

Attachment to worldly experiences leads to suffering.

The ego living inside us is mainly responsible for our continual dissatisfaction—it is what leads us to tend to focus our attention on what we lack, on the past and on the future, or on what could be a risk to our well-being. From an evolutionary point of view, it makes sense; those human beings in the past who completely ignored danger and felt completely safe and satisfied with what they had did not survive. The generations of us that have survived until modern times are the ones who are programmed to be somewhat paranoid and to never trust completely.

The practice of Buddhism aims to reprogram our ego in order to free us from suffering or *dukkha*.

Buddhism came to Japan around the end of the Kofun Period (300 to 552 CE) and spread quickly. Religious syncretization led to the Shintoist worshiping of *kami* and Buddhism's cult of Buddhas or *hotoke* being functionally inseparable. This syncretic bonding process between Buddhism and Shinto is known in Japanese by the word *shinbutsu-shūgō* ("union of *kami* and Buddhas").

People began to make statues of many *kami*—which in ancient Shinto did not usually have a physical form—when they came to be considered part of the Buddhist cosmology. As a result, they began to acquire anthropomorphic outlines.

The earliest written references to the *kami* were recorded in the *Kojiki* and the *Nihon Shoki* in the eighth century CE. Over the following years, the *shinbutsu-shūgō* gradually added figures from Buddhism to the *kami* and this syncretic mixture was adopted by Japan's imperial family. The *shinbutsu-shūgō* officially concluded with the separation order for Shinto and Buddhism in the year 1886, giving rise to the *shinbutsu-bunri* ("separation of Buddhism and Shinto").

Although they were technically separated, the two religions coexist in relative harmony and it is difficult to understand one without the other.

It is an overgeneralization, but something I have heard both Shintoist monks and Buddhists say is this: Shinto commemorates life and Buddhism takes care of dealing with death.

Baptisms (*miyamari*) and weddings are usually celebrated in Shintoist shrines. On the other hand, funerals are carried out in Buddhist temples, which are also responsible for maintaining cemeteries.

In this aspect, I have also become just another Japanese. I have celebrated my wedding and those of friends and relatives in Shintoist shrines and attended the funerals of several members of my wife's family in Buddhist temples.

Now when I visit Buddhist temples I enter a state of introspection, perhaps contemplating my own mortality. On the other hand, when I pass through the *torii* gate of a *jinja* I feel a certain sense of awe at the universe and the surrounding nature.

In today's Shintoist shrines we can see a variety of direct Buddhist influences; it is commonplace to find the following elements: the *rōmon* (楼門, tower gate), the *haiden* (拝殿, place of worship for making offerings), the *kairō* (回廊, columned corridor), the *tōrō* (灯籠 stone lantern), and the *komainu* (狛犬, or lion dogs).

Stone lanterns are originally an architectural element of Buddhist temples that over the course of the centuries has also come to be used in Shintoist shrines.

Shinto	Buddhism
Statues of animals and mythological beasts.	Statues *(hotoke)* with human form, depicting the *Amida Butsu*. Most of them are seated in the lotus position. They also make use of statues of animals and beasts.
Simple architecture with straight lines.	Ornamental architecture, curved lines in the roofs.
Torii gates.	*Mon* gates.
Kami worship.	Worship of Buddhas or *hotoke* (people or gods who have reached *satori*).
Very primitive mythology.	More complex mythology. For example, the idea of the existence of heaven and hell came to Japan through Buddhism.

"Before the advent of Buddhism, there was no idea of a heaven or a hell. The ghosts of the departed were thought of as constant presences, needing propitiation, and able in some way to share the pleasures and the pains of the living. They required food and drink and light; and in return for these; they could confer benefits. Their bodies had melted into earth; but their spirit-power still lingered in the upper world, thrilled its substance, moved in its winds and waters. By death they had acquired mysterious force; they had become 'superior ones,' Kami, gods."

– Lafcadio Hearn, *Japan: An Attempt at Interpretation*

Confucianism

"To continue and preserve is power."

– Japanese proverb

Confucian thinking is fundamental to an understanding of Asia. The work *Analects*, a compilation of proverbs and conversations attributed to Confucius (551 BCE–479 BCE), sets forth his philosophy. Chapter XV, verse 24 presents his version of the Golden Rule:

Zi Gong asked, saying, "Is there one word which may serve as a rule of practice for all one's life?"

The Master said, "Is not RECIPROCITY such a word? What you do not want done to yourself, do not do to others."[16]

This "negative form" of the Golden Rule is also known as the Silver Rule, since it does not suppose that we have to do anything for others—it simply dissuades us from carrying out acts that may harm others.

Whereas the Golden Rule laid out in the Gospel of Matthew (New Testament) urges us to act proactively:

---

[16] Translation extracted from the Chinese Text Project, https://ctext.org/analects/wei-ling-gong

*Therefore, whatever you desire for men to do to you, you shall
also do to them; for this is the law and the prophets.*
(Matthew 7:12)

The way that the government is organized, the emphasis
on maintaining harmony both within families and society, and
the worshiping of ancestors above all, are aspects of Japanese
culture inherited from the influence of Confucianism.

Here are some more ethical cornerstones fostered by Confucianism that helped to constitute the governments of the first
Chinese dynasties and over time also spread into Japan:

- In order to achieve peace, harmony and social order, it is
  necessary for each individual to behave well and virtuous-
  ly, abiding by the rules and complying with honor.
- People's education from childhood is of crucial importance
  in order to build a good society.
- Respect and honor our ancestors.
- Maintain harmony in the "five types of relationships": cit-
  izen and state, mother/father and children, husband and
  wife, between siblings, and between friends.

The five most important virtues are: benevolence (*ren* 仁),
justice (*yi* 義), ritualism (*li* 禮), wisdom (*zhi* 智), and integrity
(*xin* 信).

The sense of honor and duty that compels citizens to abide
by the rules contributes greatly to the low crime levels in China,
Japan and Korea. A negative consequence of the importance of
honor is a feeling of excessive social pressure, which in turn
fosters a society in which making mistakes or failing is looked
down on, since you run the risk of being humiliated. As mentioned earlier, the anthropologist Ruth Benedict argued in her
book *The Chrysanthemum and the Sword* that Japanese behavior
and morality is principally dominated by "shame culture." That
is to say, social harmony is maintained thanks to the fear of being judged by others and consequently feeling shame. Benedict
maintains that in other regions of the world, people's behavior

is principally led by "guilt culture"; members of society avoid acting in an immoral way out of fear of feeling guilty.

Taoism

Just as *Shinto* translates as "the path of the *kami*," Taoism or Daoism may be translated as "the path to God," but often the literature of this philosophy simply refers to "the path." The Chinese for Taoism is *dàojiào* and is written 道教, whereby the first character means "path" and the second "to learn" or "doctrine." The *Tao Te Ching*, the most important book in Taoism, teaches us that to follow the path, it is crucial to find harmony and balance both on a personal level and as a family, group or society. This book teaches us to accept that life is full of contradictions and dualities: the *ying* must be complemented by the *yang*, black by white, good contrasts with evil, work needs rest, stress is balanced by relaxation, after something savory we desire something sweet…

Another fundamental principle of Taoism is *wu wei*. This is one of the philosophical bases for martial arts like Japanese judo or aikido and for nearly all the varieties of Chinese *wushu* (Kung fu). *Wu wei* asserts that the most appropriate way to confront something is to "act effortlessly." That might be interpreted as meaning that the best way to solve a problem is to do nothing, but that is not the message it aims to convey. The true lesson of *wu wei* is that the best strategy is usually to follow the most natural course of action, the one requiring the least effort to solve a tricky situation.

Water flows along a river, adapting itself to the natural course of the meanders. When it meets with some resistance, erosion helps it to find new paths. Another often-used metaphor is that of bamboo, which flexes when the wind blows, but does not snap. We have all had the experience of things not going well for us when we have forced a solution or adopted a contrived attitude.

"Act without doing. Work without effort. Think of the small as large and the few as many. Confront the difficult and it will be easy."

— *Tao Te Ching* Section 63

For water and bamboo, acting in accordance with *wu wei* is simple, but how about for us humans? What is the "natural" rhythm in our jobs? What is the "natural" way to solve a conflict with our partner? What is the "natural" pressure we should bring to bear in a negotiation?

Nowadays, the search for the preservation of harmony through avoiding conflict, especially in the business context, is something that China, Korea and Japan have in common. If we are negotiating with an Asian company, it is a good idea not to force the situation and to be patient. For example, while in Western corporations the most important thing is typically greater financial gain and implementing (a deal) as fast as possible, for them the number one priority is to not endanger their long-term reputation and to consider the risks of a new business relationship.

Taoism came to Japan in the fifth and sixth centuries, and over time was officially recognized as *onmyōdō* (the way of the *ying* and the *yang*). *Onmyōdō* had many premonitory elements and esoteric practices for combating evil spirits and in the year 1870 was abolished by the government.

Protective talismans (*ofuda, omamori*) are one of the legacies of *onmyōdō* that have been conserved and can be seen today, both in Shintoist shrines and in Buddhist temples. If you visit a shrine or temple, the talismans are normally on sale near the entrance. Next to each *ofuda* and *omamori* there is usually an English translation that explains the type of protection it affords to whoever should possess it.

It is traditional to return the talisman after some time (normally a year) to the same shrine where you bought it. If it is not possible for you to go back to the place where you bought it, some shrines allow you to return talismans from other sites and also accept mailed returns.

"Life is a series of natural spontaneous changes. Don't resist them; that only creates sorrow. Let reality be reality. Let things flow naturally forward in whatever way they like."

— Lao Tzu

CHAPTER **7**

MORALITY AND PHILOSOPHY

ဆာ•လ

"To do good is to be pure.
To commit evil is to be impure."
— Shintoist proverb

Nature

One of the fundamental principles of the Shintoist cosmovision is the consideration that stones, rivers, mountains, trees, animals, and any other natural element, contain a divine essence. We humans also possess divinity, and among the *kami* there is no hierarchy other than a genealogical one.

In other words, from the point of view of the essence of our existence, we are all "equal" or made up of "the same." We are simply different aspects of the universe.

Using the mathematical symbol "greater than" > to indicate superiority, and "equals" = to indicate equality, these are some of the typical ways in which we tend to classify the essence of what exists in the universe:

God > Humanity > Nature
Gods > Humanity > Nature
Humanity > Nature
Humanity = Nature
Kami = Humanity = Nature

The last formula on the list is the one that corresponds to Shinto. If we substitute *kami* for *hotoke* or *bodhisattva*, it can also be applied to some Buddhist traditions and shamanic religions.

In Greek mythology, Gaia is the personification of our planet. Her equivalent in Rome was the goddess Terra. In Homer's *Iliad*, a black lamb is sacrificed and offered to her. In Hesiod's poetry, she takes on human form and plays an important role as Zeus' nurse. Sophocles described Gaia as *pamvōtis* ("the one who nurtures us all").

In the 1970s, the chemist James Lovelock proposed the Gaia Hypothesis. The idea behind this was that planet Earth should be considered an entity or organism that emerges, evolves and changes thanks to all the elements living together on it. That is, the organisms living on the planet, including us, evolve together with the Earth—she changes us and we change her. Moreover, the Earth is a complex self-regulating system, composed of both organic and inorganic material, and each one of the creatures that exists or has existed has contributed to the current state of the planet. Although our instinct is to fight for our survival, it is nevertheless impossible for us to live alone; when the day comes for us to start living on Mars, one of the first things we will need to do to survive is to plant potatoes.

The Gaia metaphor aligns with the cosmovision of many religions, among them Buddhism and Shinto. Shinto would have it that the ideal good life consists of living in harmony with our environment. In some cultures, this may simply mean that we must respect nature, but there's more to it.

We have a certain tendency to think we humans are superior to all other creatures, and that therefore it is our mission to protect the forests. But the Japanese vision goes further; it is also important for the forests and other living creatures to take care of us. It is a reciprocal, symbiotic relationship in which no one and nothing is superior to anyone/anything else.

Let's analyze that subtle difference through architecture.

My first visit to a town outside of Tokyo when I came to Japan was to Nikko. One of the things that most surprised me was how the town was laid out. In Spain, and also in most places in Europe, we are used to villages and towns with a square at their heart with a church and/or city hall. Streets tend to radiate out from the center, which is surrounded by buildings and houses. The most sacred place—a church or cathedral—is as separated as possible from nature.

With my preconceived ideas, I was expecting Nikko to be a town with shrines and temples in a central square and streets around it protecting them. But when I got there, I came across straight streets facing a mountain covered by a leafy forest. I walked along the main street, with houses and buildings on both sides, until I reached the hillside. There, after I had crossed the bridge over the river Daiya, I plunged into the oak and cedar forest. As I went on, enveloped by mist, I made out the silhouette of a pagoda, which could have been just another tree. Further on, I headed into the Toshogu shrine complex and spent the day strolling around the woods, temples and shrines.

With this experience in Nikko, I began to understand the big difference a change of perspective can make: instead of marking a clear separation between artificial and natural things, the aim is to integrate the two worlds. Even bang in the middle of the capital city, the most important shrines are surrounded by forests (*chinju no mori*) and it is difficult to define a place as the "main square" or "center" of Tokyo since most of the downtown area is occupied by the gardens of the Imperial Palace.

This integrative philosophy may be observed in Japanese architecture too, especially in traditional wood houses. The walls are usually thin, which can be a disadvantage in the winter, but helps to cope with the humidity of Japanese summers. What I most like about sleeping in a traditional thin-walled Japanese house is that I can clearly hear the sounds of nature; depending on the season, you can hear frogs croaking, crickets chirping, the wind stirring the bamboo canes, the rain hitting the roof...

The *engawa* verandas are designed in such a way that if you open a room's sliding screens, you almost get the feeling of being in the garden. The only thing separating the *engawa* from the gravel or lawn is the raised wood deck.

Engawa are wooden verandas raised slightly above the grounds of a garden.

The design of Japanese gardens is also different to that of Western ones. The Japanese garden tries to imitate nature: the paths are marked out with stones on the ground, the vegetation is placed asymmetrically, rigid forms are avoided when pruning trees, and moss is allowed to grow on the rocks.

The dry garden of Ryoan-ji in Kyoto is a classic example. It is a mostly gravel-covered area, with fifteen moss-covered rocks arranged asymmetrically. Walking in it is not permitted but visitors may sit on the temple's wooden floor to contemplate it.

Meanwhile, Western gardens tend to try to impose order and symmetry; paths are usually laid out in a regular and orderly fashion, hedges are trimmed to create well-defined shapes, fountains and (normally human) sculptures adorn the place, the vegetation is pruned so that it doesn't invade certain limits marked out with fences, etc.

The Gardens of Versailles are an emblematic example of the Western garden. Designed by André Le Nôtre, they have geometric flower beds, trimmed hedges, and numerous fountains and sculptures. The grandeur of the design reflects the power and wealth of Louis XIV.

Western thinking	Traditional Japan
Tendency toward the separation of natural and artificial things	Integration and symbiosis of artificial and natural things
Cities and villages built around a central square normally presided over by a sacred building.	Cities and villages tend not to have a defined form. Sacred buildings are usually surrounded by green areas or located in forests.
Houses with an imposing facade.	Traditional houses that seek symbiosis with the surrounding environment. It is sometimes difficult to make out the façade.
There is a tendency to try to impress.	The aim is to be in harmony with the natural environment and to create an atmosphere of peace.

Good and Evil, the Pure and the Contaminated

In Shinto there is no absolute good or evil; no one and nothing is perfect. It could be categorized as a type of moral or ethical relativism.

This way of thinking permeates Japanese society at all levels: legal system, government, businesses.... To judge whether an act is good or bad, they take into account the context, circumstances, intention, etc. Seen through the prism of other cultures, this relativism can lead to conflicts in international relations or in the business world.

On a personal level, we can see it as a fundamentally optimistic faith, as it believes that humans are born good and that evil is caused by evil spirits who lead us to act in bad faith.

The purpose of most of the Shintoist rituals we saw in Chapter 5 is to ward off evil spirits through purification, prayers and offerings to the *kami*. The purity of our spirit and kindness is dependent on our actions. One of Shinto's fundamental precepts is that to do good is to be pure; to commit evil is to be impure.

Good is synonymous with purity. Evil is synonymous with contamination or corruption (*kegare*: 汚れ).

One of the recurring themes in Japanese literature, cinema, anime and manga is that the main character or hero is usually the one with the purest heart. But sometimes the good guys become bad and vice versa. That is, certain events lead to "evil" or "kindness" being transferred from some characters to others.

In Haruki Murakami's *Kafka on the Shore*, the character Tamura kills his father because an evil spirit evil dwells inside him. Nakata, another of the novel's important characters, also turns out to be a killer and murders a man called Johnnie Walker. Both of them have a series of adventures and encounters with other people that help them break free from evil.

"The border between good and evil is terribly fuzzy."
– Milan Kundera

Why do we have to remove our shoes before entering a house in Japan?

However clean your shoes might be, it is rude to enter a house without taking them off. As well as being a question of hygiene, this is also because there are "spirits" or "dirtiness" outside that may have contaminated you. If you step inside a house with this footwear, you might be bringing the bad luck into the home. Hence the importance of taking off your shoes or using a pair of *surippa* (slippers).

Wakeiseijaku

Wakeiseijaku is a fundamental concept in the Japanese tea ceremony. This term is composed of four characters representing essential principles for the practice of the tea ceremony and also for life in Japan.

Let's take a look at what each character means:

1. **Wa (和)**: Harmony. This principle emphasizes the importance of peace and tranquility in all relationships and activities. In the tea ceremony, the aim is to create a harmonious atmosphere between the host and guests, and also with nature and the objects used in the ceremony.

2. **Kei (敬)**: Respect. Mutual respect and consideration for others is one of the most important values of Japanese culture. In the tea ceremony, respect is shown in every single action and detail, from the preparation of the tea to the way in which the guests and utensils are treated. My last master of ceremonies said to me: "Touch the cup as though it were the hands of the person you most love."

3. **Sei (清)**: Purity. This principle refers both to physical and spiritual purity. In the tea ceremony, great emphasis is placed on cleanliness and the order in which each utensil is placed. Purity also implies sincerity and honesty in human interactions.

4. **Jaku (寂)**: Tranquility. Inner calm and serenity. In the tea ceremony, the aim is to reach a state of tranquility and inner peace, distancing yourself from the hubbub and worries of the outside world.

Wa 和 (Harmony)

One of the oldest names for what we know today as Japan was *wa*. Prince Shōtoku (574–622), inspired by what he learned from Confucian and Buddhist philosophers from China, wrote in the first article of the constitution that *wa* 和 (peace and harmony) should take precedence as the most important value ahead of all else.

The use of the character 和 has endured through history up until the present day. From the year 2019, with the change of Emperor, we began a new era in Japan called *reiwa* 令和 (令: to maintain, 和: peace). The year 2025 corresponds to Year 7 of the *reiwa* era.

Having the aim of living with harmony by avoiding conflicts is one of the fundamental values of Japanese culture.

Subconsciously, both with the individual Japanese and with society at large, the default tendency is to act in a non-confrontational way. An example I gave in my book *A Geek in Japan* that serves to illustrate this type of behavior is that of a customer who asks for tickets for a specific bullet train journey, but it turns out there are no seats left. The way the person who is dealing with you responds may be confusing if you are not used to Japanese manners. In general, they will not give you a direct answer like: "there are no tickets left" but instead will soften it by saying something more indirect, like: "It appears the seats available at this time are limited, but we have seats at this other time."

Similar reactions are also typical and happen frequently when you ask for something extra or unavailable in a restaurant, hotel, or shop. If you interpret this type of answer literally, it seems to have a double meaning and can cause confusion and even frustration to someone coming from a culture with a more "confrontational" and direct kind of communication.

It is hard for them to give a straight "no," but in the twenty years I have been here, I have noticed a slight change toward a more direct style of communication, perhaps due to the arrival of new generations of young Japanese or the increase in foreign tourism.

Makoto まこと (Sincerity)

"Sincerity is the mother of knowledge."
– Japanese proverb

Makoto translates as "sincerity" or "authenticity" and is regarded as one of the fundamental values of Shinto.

Unlike other religions, there is no formal process in which a person becomes a Shintoist or stops being one. Anyone may visit a shrine and pray with *makoto* (sincerity from the depths of one's heart) to join with the divine.

Making a mistake with the intricate ways of carrying out a bow or making a wish is no big thing; what matters is showing respect and authenticity.

In Japanese literature, manga and anime, a static lead character (that remains unchanged throughout the whole story) is commonplace; they always act honestly and as a result serve as agents of change for other characters.

Luffy, the main character in *One Piece*, is optimistic and good-humored. His character and motivation (he ends up becoming the King of the Pirates) remain stable throughout the whole story. But his cheerful outlook inspires both allies and enemies to stop doing bad things and to act kindly.

In the novel *Snow Country*, by Yasunari Kawabata, the main character Shimamura is also a static character but with his *makoto*-filled words he gradually changes the attitude to life of both the geisha Komako and the young Yoko.

The sincerity and honesty of our actions has the capacity to change the people who accompany us in life.

"The first and surest means to enter into communion with the Divine is sincerity."
– Japanese proverb

CHAPTER 8

SHINTO-INSPIRED PRACTICES FOR EVERYDAY LIFE

ℰ❀ℬ

"Everyone makes mistakes. Nobody's perfect."
— Japanese proverb

Over the last few decades, we have learned from Buddhist traditions that the practice of different types of meditation can benefit our health. Mindfulness is practiced by millions of people, and is used in clinics and hospitals all over the world. India and China have brought us yoga and *qi gong* too—practices that integrate taking care of the body and mind.

In the case of Shinto, it is more difficult to point to a concrete practice we can incorporate directly. But there are several ideas and concepts we can use as inspiration to improve our lives.

Less Is More

Shinto architecture tends to eschew ornaments; *honden* don't even have doors or windows and the simplest *torii* gates are two wooden columns and a lintel. Only that which is essential is used to build a shrine. The principles of Shinto architecture inspired the minimalism that permeated the product design industry in Japanese companies in the first postwar decades.

Steve Jobs, who traveled to Japan many times throughout his life, took inspiration from the simplicity and essentiality of Japanese industrial design to lay the foundations of the Apple ethos. The culmination of this way of thinking was the invention of the smartphone.

At the time when Steve Jobs proposed the iPhone in the early twenty-first century, many people probably said to him: "A telephone without buttons?"; "You're crazy! That's impossible." But it turned out Steve Jobs was right—buttons are not the essential thing in a phone, the only thing you need is a screen.

On a personal level, sometimes a little voice says to us: "Impossible! I can't live without alcohol."; "I can't live without my favorite cookies every morning."; "I can't live without X." But in reality, we CAN live perfectly well without X, just as it is possible to create a telephone without buttons.

It is not easy to fight against that little voice.

Becoming attached to objects and always wanting more is programmed into our genes. In the past, accumulating food and resources was paramount to survival. Now we live in an age of abundance, where it is hard for us to differentiate between what is essential and what is not. We keep on wanting ever more things, but instead of accumulating food, we consume infinite digital information on our screens. Social networks and streaming services offering us series and movies trick our limbic system into feeling we never have enough.

The bombardment of information and options sidetracks us from what is important—from our path.

If you keep on pouring hot water into a cup that is already filled to the brim, you will end up spilling it and staining the table. Empty the cup before refilling it.

To not desire anything is to have everything; the one who desires everything has nothing.

> *"He who chases after two rabbits will catch neither."*
> – Japanese proverb[17]

---

[17] Original in Japanese: "*Nito wo oumono ha itto mo ezu*, 二兎を追う者は一兎をも得ず。"

Adding Space—*Ma* 間

"In linked verse, put your mind to what is not."
– Shinsei, fifteenth century poet

One of the Japanese aesthetic values inherited from Shinto and from Zen Buddhism is the idea that empty space is just as or more important than its "container." That is, the empty space enclosed by walls or a fence is beautiful and has meaning without any need to add anything. The concept is also applied to the blank space on works of art, to the silences in musical pieces and to the intervals when nothing particular happens in a movie and the story does not move forward.

More examples where *ma* 間 plays a role: the stones encircled by *shimenawa* ropes in a Shintoist shrine, the gravel of a Zen garden, the *tatamis* with no table or chairs in a *tokonoma* (traditional Japanese room), the unpainted areas (negative space) in a painting or statue, the pauses in theater actors' movements and what they don't say, what is left unsaid in a novel, the lack of explanations in a *haiku*, the separation between each branch and leaf in a floral arrangement (*ikebana*)…

If you are an artist, thinking about what you subtract, eliminate from, or leave unsaid in your works of art will help you project a new dimension of meaning onto them.

In everyday life, we can also experiment with *ma*:

- Throw out furniture or junk from a room or corner of your home where you tend to collect things you don't normally use. In the space you acquire add a *tatami* or a rug.
- Keep your hands off your electronic devices and stroll around a park or mountain wherever your legs take you.
- Organize a vacation in the countryside.
- Spend a Sunday without looking at any screens—no TV, cell phone or computer.
- Establish a corner or room of your home to be kept free of objects or decorations.

- Devote an afternoon to throwing away, recycling or selling objects you don't need.
- Clean up your computer's desktop or get rid of apps you don't use on your smartphone.
- Take a year off.
- Go three days without looking at your email in-box.
- Don't eat anything for breakfast—just have a cup of tea.

Hot Water Baths—Ofuro

In Chapter 5 we learned about the importance of purification rituals (*misogi*) using elements like water or salt. A simple way to emulate *misogi* is by taking a bath.

The Japanese custom of bathing in hot springs goes back to the seventh and eighth centuries. In manuscripts from as far back as the Heian Period (794–1185), shrines with public hot springs are mentioned where people would go to bathe. During the Edo Period (1603–1868), bathtubs (*ofuro*) began to be installed in houses. Nowadays, taking a bath is a daily habit for many Japanese. The usual custom is to bathe for around twenty minutes in hot water (between 100 to 108 degrees Fahrenheit or 38 and 42 degrees Celsius) before going to bed.

Some of the benefits of a hot bath:
- It improves your sleep.
- It improves your blood circulation.
- It cleans your skin's pores.
- It relaxes your muscles.
- It alleviates joint pain.

Engraving by Utagawa Toyokuni showing an everyday
scene in a public bathhouse from the Edo Period.

Kotodama

Kotodama (言: word, 霊: spirit) is the Japanese belief that words and names can have mystical powers. The enunciation of *kotodama* may influence and produce changes in the real world.

In the *Kojiki* (*Records of Ancient Matters*), the deities Amaterasu and Susanoo say: "Let each of us swear, and produce children." Moments after uttering these words, Amaterasu gives birth to five gods.

In Hayao Miyazaki's movie *Spirited Away*, one of the key moments in the plot is when the witch Yubaba changes the name of the leading character from Chihiro to Sen. This spell symbolizes the loss of Chihiro's original identity.

At the end of the movie, Chihiro remembers her full name, and also helps Haku remember his real name. This act of remembering their names and saying them out loud allows the two characters to recover their true identities and free themselves from Yubaba's spells and escape her control.

In the movie *Laputa: Castle in the Sky*, also directed by Hayao Miyazaki, the idea that *kotodama* can have special powers also plays a crucial role in the narrative. The charm worn by Sheeta, the main character, reacts to certain words. Sheeta pronounces a verse her mother taught her and suddenly a sleeping robot is activated that protects her from a military attack.

At the end of the movie, Sheeta and Pazu recite a spell together to destroy the city of Laputa. Not only do they manage to destroy the city, but they also free themselves from the "corrupting influence" (*kegare*) that others are trying to exert on them.

The words of the spells activated by the charm's powers are more than just sounds; they are imbued with power and meaning.

One of the movie's aims is to make us see the importance of knowledge and traditions being handed down from generation to generation. Stories, verses and words have the power to preserve history and culture.

The main character in Haruki Murakami's novel *Kafka on the Shore*—Kafka Tamura—faces an inner journey of self-discovery and understanding of his identity. The name "Kafka" itself is a word loaded with meaning and partly determines the character's destiny. Moreover, the words to the song "Kafka on the Shore" act as a catalyst for change in those who hear them. The song's lyrics trigger memories and emotions that have a profound impact on the characters.

In *1Q84*, another of Haruki Murakami's novels, the two main characters Aomame and Tengo find themselves in a world that is an alternative version of the year 1984. This reality is referred to as "1Q84," with the "Q" representing "question," symbolizing the uncertainty and differences between the two dimensions. The existence of this alternative reality may be seen as a manifestation of the power of words and ideas to create new realities. Tengo is a writer and editor who is rewriting a novel titled *The Air Chrysalis*. The novel within the novel acts as a prophecy.

Neurolinguistic programming (a methodology that uses language to improve our behavior) suggests that the words we use have the power to influence our subconscious and also the way we act. If we say negative things like "I can't do X" we are stalling ourselves and we won't take action. But if we say "I'm learning to do X" that will most probably motivate us to begin to learn to do X. Another example would be to change "I'm a failure" for "I'm in a process of learning and growth."

Being more aware of the words we say to other people and also of our internal dialog is the starting point for "reprogramming ourselves." Instead of seeing a bump in the road as unsolvable, we can regard it as an opportunity. Instead of beating ourselves up when we get things wrong, it is better to consider our errors as ideal learning opportunities.

For example, if the markets fall, many people start to panic and sell at a loss, but the best strategy is usually to take advantage of slumps as ideal investment opportunities. The Japanese word for crisis is *kiki* 危機, the first character 危 means "danger" and the second one 機 means "opportunity." Hiroto Kiritani, a famous Japanese investor, says that he always buys shares when they have dropped to their lowest level in 52 weeks.

As well as being a vehicle for communication, human language also has the capacity to influence the way we see the world. Proactive language and positive words drive us to act correctly; on the other hand, negativity depresses and paralyzes us.

The belief that words may have a liberating, divine, healing power is not unique to Japanese culture—Hinduism and Buddhism believe in the power of mantras.

The Gospel according to John begins like this:

In the beginning was the Word, and the Word was with God, and the Word was God. He was with God in the beginning. Through him all things were made; without him nothing was made that has been made. In him was life, and that life was the light of all mankind. The light shines in the darkness, and the darkness has not overcome it.

There was a man sent from God whose name was John. He came as a witness to testify concerning that light, so that through him all might believe. He himself was not the light; he came only as a witness to the light.

The true light that gives light to everyone was coming into the world. He was in the world, and though the world was made through him, the world did not recognize him.

Rituals Are More Important Than Objectives

The de-ritualization (disappearance of rituals) of society is one of the problems the world has been facing over the last few decades.

The disappearance of established routines doesn't go down well with us. Nearly all of us noticed this negative effect during the pandemic, when the structure of our days was shattered. The lack of routines or extreme changes causes us stress.

I use the words "ritual" and "habit" as synonyms to refer to simple acts we repeat each day: having breakfast, going out for a coffee, driving to the office, getting on the subway, working for a few hours, attending meetings, answering phone calls, always going for a walk at the same time, going for the newspaper, going to see a soccer game, studying, reading while sitting in our favorite armchair, etc. When something or someone interrupts one of our personal rituals, it usually puts us in a bad mood, especially in the morning.

Automating tasks, activities or work that we have to carry out repeatedly is a good idea since it avoids us having to be constantly taking decisions. Various psychology studies[18] came to the conclusion that decision taking tires us out. They say that one of the reasons why CEOs of large companies (like Steve Jobs or Mark Zuckerberg) always dress the same is because they don't want to have to choose which clothes to wear each morning.

On the other hand, as we get older we tend to pick up harmful habits. Reprogramming bad habits is not easy—there are entire books devoted to it. In *The Ikigai Journey* (Tuttle Publishing), my coauthor Francesc Miralles and I devoted several chapters to specific techniques for replacing bad habits with other more healthful ones. There is no one-size-fits-all solution—the important thing is to try out different techniques in order to get to know our inclinations and, over time, learn what works best for us.

---

[18] "Do You Suffer from Fatigue?" by John Tierney. *New York Times Magazine*. https://www.nytimes.com/2011/08/21/magazine/do-you-suffer-from-decision-fatigue.html

As a general strategy we want:
- To eliminate negative habits.
- To add positive ones.

That is easier said than done because our natural tendency is to fall into habits and to stick with them regardless of whether or not they are good or bad. These are some of the most popular methods:

1. Rewarding ourselves

This technique consists of giving ourselves a reward each time we manage to complete a new habit successfully. Examples: we can only watch an episode of our favorite series once we have finished studying ten pages for our next exam, or we will only eat a dessert if previously we have taken some exercise.

2. Changing our identity

Popularized by James Clear, this technique consists of changing the way we see ourselves. If you self-identify as a lazy, silly or fat person it is very difficult to introduce habits that might make you more productive, intelligent or thin. Our identity is usually formed over the years and is highly susceptible to what other people say about us. If they often say to us that we are bad at math, we will end up believing this and lose all interest in the subject. If they tell us we are fat, we will end up accepting that this is who we are and we will neglect our diet. On the other hand, if we self-identify as a person who is fit and very healthy, when we get to a restaurant we will tend to choose healthy food in order to be consistent with our identity.

3. Ritual chaining

A lot of willpower is needed in order to get down to taking exercise at any time of day or night. But it is relatively easy to decide that we should always do ten minutes of exercise before getting a shower. Examples of chaining: having a cup of tea, taking exercise, having a shower, having a snack, or reading for half an hour. On the Internet, "morning routines" or "night routines" are all the rage. If you search for those terms online, you will find a plethora of ideas to create your own "habit or ritual chains."

4. Incremental: change one habit incrementally instead of trying for a radical change

If we have a negative habit, getting rid of it by going "cold turkey" is possible but difficult. If you want to wake up two hours earlier and you start by directly setting your alarm clock two hours earlier, it's likely that after a few days you will not be able to sustain this change. It is better to begin with ten-minute increments as you gradually get used to the new wake-up time each morning. If you want to lose a lot of weight, starting a radical diet to try to lose a lot of weight in one month will probably lead to failure. It is better to begin by changing your dinner or breakfast, cutting down on amounts or replacing desserts with something that has fewer calories.

5. The 21-day rule

It is said that we need 21 days to make a new habit become something automatic that we have no difficulty in repeating. Personally, I have tried several times to add a new routine to my life for 21 days in a row, but subsequently didn't manage to keep it up. New studies say that we need an average of 66 days[19] and that the time needed to create a new habit varies depending on the person and the type of change.

In Japanese society they tend to value rituals above objectives. They are both important but more emphasis is placed on improving those habits or processes which are repeated (and improving them through *kaizen*) in order to reach the objectives.

---

[19] *How Are Habits Formed: Modelling Habit Formation in the Real World* by Phillippa Lally et al. *European Journal of Social Psychology.* https://onlinelibrary.wiley.com/doi/abs/10.1002/ejsp.674

This way of working can be observed in companies, educational institutions, government, services, sports, etc.

When I worked in the cell phone industry I had the chance to visit smartphone factories both in the United States and in Japan. In the American installations I noticed that the annual objectives and even the daily ones were of paramount importance, but on the assembly lines they did not pay as much attention to detail as they did in the Shizuoka factories.

I gave up writing down my New Year's resolutions—now I *describe*: rituals that I want to introduce, ones that I want to eliminate and others that I want to improve. Once I have written down the rituals, I categorize them and for each category I assign a final objective. In other words, I do not ignore the objectives, but first of all I focus on deciding on the habits that will lead to me achieving them.

For example, in January I noted down in my diary:

- Each day before going to sleep I have to read books about the history of Shinto and take notes.
- Each day as soon as I get up I have to write at least 500 words for my forthcoming book about Shinto.
- Each evening just after having dinner I have to edit the manuscript of the book.

Next, I grouped them in the "Spirit of Shinto" category. Following these three rituals would help me over time to achieve my objective of finishing this book.

For artists, enjoying the creative process is more important than the final result. In fact, I believe that the artists who enjoy themselves the most when they're working are the ones who end up producing the best works.

Rituals help us to add structure and order to the chaos which tends to take control of our lives.

Rituals come before objectives.

Micro Rituals

One of the typical problems of trying to introduce changes to our daily life is that we only achieve them for a short time. The idea of micro rituals is that they have to be habits which are sufficiently "micro" to be able to be incorporated fairly effortlessly. For example, if we don't read anything, a micro ritual would be to read one page of a book each day. If we want to walk more, a micro ritual would be to walk 500 steps more than the average that we normally walk.

This is my current list of micro rituals or micro rules:
- To walk at least 10,000 steps a day (last year I would walk 9,500).
- To read five pages from a novel in Japanese each day (I'm only in the habit of reading manga in Japanese and I want to improve my vocabulary by reading novels).
- To answer three e-mails a day (I lost the habit of looking at my e-mail due to health problems).

Create your list of micro rituals. If you begin to fail, make adjustments so that you can carry them out. Do not be ambitious. The idea of micro rituals is that they should be so easy as to be able to be carried out without hardly any effort. Merely achieving something reinforces our brain's reward mechanism[20] and motivates us to go on doing it.

---

[20] Brain's reward system https://en.wikipedia.org/wiki/Reward_system

Reconnect With the Rhythm of Nature

*"Even in one single leaf on a tree, or in one blade of grass,
the awesome Deity presents itself."*

— Shintoist proverb

In the book *Forest Bathing: the Rejuvenating Practice of Shinrin Yoku*, Francesc Miralles and I talked about how important it is to keep our connection with nature given that it has healing properties. When we stroll through green areas, forests and parks we breathe in phytoncides, which plants and trees give off. Phytoncides are particles that have a strengthening effect on the immune system (they increase NK cell activity) and reduce stress (they decrease cortisol levels).

If we live in a city, far from nature, we miss out on those benefits. In these cases, it is a good idea to make walks around urban parks or getaways to the countryside a part of our lifestyle.

Whenever you find yourself in a natural environment, breathe in deeply and take a few moments to appreciate the beauty and awe of what is around you. You are part of nature.

Can you feel the *"kami*ness" that lives in trees, plants, rivers, animals and rocks?

Hayao Miyazaki's message—we are nature's companions

One of the recurring themes in Hayao Miyazaki's movies (and those of other Studio Ghibli directors) is the contrast between the role of nature and what is created by modern society. Hayao Miyazaki rejects the notion that humanity is on a higher plane than nature; for him, there is no superiority or inferiority—we are simply inseparable companions of the natural world.

This vision is in alignment with the Shintoist cosmovision according to which humanity is an inseparable part of nature.

In Miyazaki's movies the landscapes are alive.

In the movie *Princess Mononoke,* the Cedar Forest is home to the Shishigami (a deer *kami* that has an almost human face), thousands of friendly-looking entities also dwell there. To depict the forest, Hayao Miyazaki took inspiration from a trip to Yakushima, an island in the south of Japan, covered by one of the country's most beautiful forests.

In the movie *My Neighbor Totoro*, the main characters Mei and Satsuki become friends with Totoro, a creature with a good-natured, kind appearance, who protects a scared tree encircled by a *shimenawa* rope. By personifying the natural world, Hayao Miyazaki makes us feel compassion and a renewed connection to nature. We would all like to have a friend like Totoro.

In *Nausicaä of the Valley of the Wind*, the Fukai forest has become a contaminated place as result of a human interference. The air in the woods is full of a toxic gas that kills almost everything except for some giant insects. It is a hellish, uninhabitable place. Humanity is capable of destroying its own soul.

"Reverence for the land lies at the very core of Shinto, the native religion, which holds that Japan's mountains, rivers, and trees are sacred, the dwelling place of gods."
— Alex Kerr, *Dogs and Demons*

Use Your Intuition to Make Decisions

"There can be as much value in the blink of an eye as in months of rational analysis."
— Malcom Gladwell

The main message of Marie Kondo's KonMari method is to encourage us to take decisions based on our intuition: if something gives us good vibes, we keep it—if it gives us bad vibes, we eliminate it. But before throwing an object out, Marie Kondo suggests to us that we should express gratitude toward it. This act of gratitude is part of the recognition that everything has a certain value in our lives, even if we are going to get rid of it. I cannot help but think that Marie Kondo is influenced by Shinto; she visualizes spirits or *kami* in objects and she herself has mentioned in her books that Shinto is one of her sources of inspiration.

The moral of Malcolm Gladwell's book *Blink: The Power of Thinking Without Thinking* is similar. He presents us with a plethora of scientific studies that have shown that human intuition is more powerful than we think it is. One of the examples Gladwell describes is that of two groups of art buyers selecting a painting to decorate the living room of their homes. The members of the first group were given the freedom to think for hours about which work to choose. However, the members of the second group were only allowed a few minutes before having to make a decision. In the days following the acquisition, those who had had more time to choose were more satisfied than those who had had to use their intuition. But when they were asked again after a few months, the ones from the quick decision group were much happier with the work of art decorating their living rooms. This experiment suggests that when we have just taken a quick decision guided by intuition, we feel some uncertainty, but once we have gotten over that phase, we are generally happier with the final result.

When in doubt, believe in your instinct.

Treat Your Home Like a Shrine

"The inside of a house or apartment after decluttering has much in common with a Shinto shrine... a place where there are no unnecessary things, and our thoughts become clear."

– Marie Kondo

One of the factors that Shinto shrines have in common is that they are simple and harmonious—there is no showiness to them. Each visit to a shrine makes us feel calm. They need nothing more and nothing less. They only have what is essential.

What if we treated our homes as though they were sacred places?

The environment where we live affects our mood. It is a good idea to devote some effort to improving the places where we spend most of our time.

Look for a corner of your home where you may create a little "you" space. It can be as simple as placing a coffee table and a chair beside a window. Adorn the table with your favorite flowers or some object that brings you good memories. Design the corner in such a way that you feel like sitting down there and relaxing, to observe your thoughts and contemplate the scenery or sky through the window. This will be your personal sanctuary.

Establish a series of rules for your personal sanctuary, such as:

- I cannot use digital devices.
- I cannot clutter the table with objects but just change one adornment for another.
- I cannot eat there but just have a cup of tea.

Harmonious, Sincere Solutions

"Even a sea bream loses its flavor when eaten alone."
— Japanese proverb[21]

If you find yourself in a delicate situation, remember the word *wa* (和: peace or harmony). Even if it takes you more time, make the effort to find a solution that benefits everyone and harms no one.

Ask yourself: which course of action has the best chance of reaching the least conflictive solution?

Remember, it is not about reaching perfect solutions—the starting point may be imperfect, but we'll gradually go about improving it. The Japanese aesthetic principle *wabi sabi* teaches us to accept imperfection as something beautiful.

As we saw in Chapter 7, *makoto* (the sincerity and purity of our heart) is one of the moral values the Japanese most appreciate. Be sincere, both with others and with yourself. The person who is easiest to lie to is yourself. Mirrors—sacred objects in Japan—symbolize sincerity, amongst other things, because it is believed they can reflect our spirit.

Follow the path of harmony, the beauty of imperfection and sincerity, *wa*, *wabi sabi* and *makoto*.

"A mirror has a clean light that reflects everything as it is. It symbolizes the stainless mind of the kami, *and at the same time is regarded as a sacred symbolic embodiment of the fidelity of the worshipper toward the* kami.*"*
— Sokyo Ono, *Shinto: The Kami Spirit World of Japan*

---

[21] Japanese original: 鯛も一人はうまからず

CHAPTER 9

TEN LIFE LESSONS

ಹಿ • ಲ

"The heart of the person before you is a mirror.
See there your own form."
— Japanese proverb

1. **Wa 和 (Harmony).**

The *kami* live in peace, provided that harmony is not broken. Prioritize harmony and peace. Before facing conflictive situations, look for ways you might solve them so that the interests and harmony of those involved take precedence.

2. **Be Flexible Like Bamboo.**

When the wind blows, bamboo bends without breaking, but at the same time its roots remain fixed. Having principles that you keep to is good, but at the same time it is good for us to learn to be flexible and accept other people's ideas.

3. **Start With Something Simple. Add Improvements Later.**

As we saw in Chapter 1, most Shinto shrines began from a simple element: a rock, a tree, a mountain. If you feel overwhelmed by a new undertaking, unexpected event or change, do not try to solve everything immediately. Simply start with the first step and don't try to be perfect from the beginning. Once you have taken the first step, it is easier to take the second, third step, etc. and to gradually solve and improve the situation bit by bit.

4. Add More Nature To Your Life.

Shinto shrines do not purport to impose themselves on nature—instead they try to integrate with it. In the case of urban areas, shrines bring nature to the city. The book *Forest Bathing: the Rejuvenating Practice of Shirin Yoku*, we explain the importance of nature for our health and how harmful it can be to live in a completely artificial environment. Add more walks around parks, green zones, mountains and nature in general.

5. Rituals > Objectives.

Establishing good routines and habits is more important than having objectives. Instead of writing down your objectives for the new year, try writing one list with habits you want to eliminate and another with beneficial habits you would like to introduce to your lifestyle.

6. Take Care Of Your Loved Ones And Your Community.

Both Confucianism and Shinto regard family, friends, ancestors and the community as crucial. Immersed in the hectic rush of work, we can easily let days and weeks go by without realizing we are not paying attention to the people around us. To avoid that happening, create a leisure diary—just like your work diary—to plan activities to spend time with your loved ones.

7. You Are Part Of The Universe And The Universe Is You.

This is a principle inherited from the religions and philosophies of ancient India, which came to Japan via Taoism. Being aware everything is connected to everything else helps you to be less arrogant, to be more respectful, and to see yourself reflected in other people's souls. If you get angry with someone, you are getting angry with yourself.

8. Imagine The *Kami* Surrounding You.

The *kami* live inside of us, just as they live inside a rock, a tree, a star or a cat. You don't need to believe in that literally—imagine spirits, *kami* or characters out of a Ghibli fantasy movie. Feeling that everything has a spirit—from ants to a box of objects—can help you to act differently. Feeling a greater connection to what is around us is important in order to lead an orderly life.

9. **Learn To Feel The Awe Of Being Alive.**

"Awe" is the word used to describe what we feel when we enter a temple, a mosque or a cathedral, when we witness a baby babbling its first words, when we contemplate a work of art, or when we get to the summit of a mountain surrounded by a beautiful landscape.

Awe is also the word used in translations of Motohisa Yamakage's books about Shinto to refer to the feeling of connection with the *kami*.

Look up at the starry sky. It is wonderful! Let yourself be carried away by the feeling of awe—that is, feel the immensity both of the universe surrounding you and of the universe inside you.

10. **Silence.**

It is easier to find answers in silence than in chaos.

> *"For Shinto, at root, is a religion not of sermons but of awe: which is a sentiment that may or may not produce words, but in either case goes beyond them."*
>
> – Joseph Campbell

> *"Yet, even amidst the hatred and carnage, life is still worth living. It is possible for wonderful encounters and beautiful things to exist."*
>
> – Hayao Miyazaki

Recommended Reading

Chamberlain, Basil Hall. *The Kojiki: Records of Ancient Matters*. Rutland, VT: Tuttle Publishing, 2005. Originally presented in 1882 and reprinted in 1919.

Chart, David. *Shinto Practice for Non-Japanese*. (Mimusubi Essays on Shinto). Independently Published, 2020.

Dunbar, Robin. *How Religion Evolved: And Why It Endures*. New York: Oxford University Press, 1922

Foster, Charles. *Wired for God? The Biology of Spiritual Experience*. London: Hodder & Stoughton, 2010.

Harris, Victor. *Shintō: the Sacred Art of Ancient Japan*. London: British Museum, 1999.

Hearn, Lafcadio. *Glimpses of Unfamiliar Japan* First Series (English Edition). Project Gutenberg. Released 2005, Updated 2020, Originally published by Houghton & Mifflin Co. and the Riverside Press in 1894. https://www.gutenberg.org/cache/epub/8130/pg8130-images.html

Morse, Edward Sylvester. *Japanese Homes and Their Surroundings*. Project Gutenberg. Released 2016. Originally published by Harper & Brothers 1889. https://www.gutenberg.org/ebooks/52868

Ono, Sokyo. *Shinto: the Kami Spirit World of Japan*. Rutland, VT: Tuttle Publishing, 2024. Originally published by Charles E Tuttle Co. Inc., 1962.

Rots, Aike P. "Sacred Forests, Sacred Nation: The Shinto Environmentalist Paradigm and the Rediscovery of 'Chinju no Mori'" *Japanese Journal of Religious Studies*. 42, No. 2 (2015) www.jstor.org/stable/43686903

Turnbull, Stephen. *Battles of the Samurai*. London: Arms and Armour Press, 1987.

Yamakage, Motohisa. *The Essence of Shinto*. New York: Kodansha USA, 2007.

Yamamoto, Yukitaka. *Kami no Michi–The Way of the Kami: The Life and Thought of a Shinto Priest*. Granite Falls: Tsubaki America Publications, 1999.

"Books to Span the East and West"

Tuttle Publishing was founded in 1832 in the small New England town of Rutland, Vermont [USA]. Our core values remain as strong today as they were then—to publish best-in-class books which bring people together one page at a time. In 1948, we established a publishing outpost in Japan—and Tuttle is now a leader in publishing English-language books about the arts, languages and cultures of Asia. The world has become a much smaller place today and Asia's economic and cultural influence has grown. Yet the need for meaningful dialogue and information about this diverse region has never been greater. Over the past seven decades, Tuttle has published thousands of books on subjects ranging from martial arts and paper crafts to language learning and literature—and our talented authors, illustrators, designers and photographers have won many prestigious awards. We welcome you to explore the wealth of information available on Asia at **www.tuttlepublishing.com.**

Published by Tuttle Publishing, an imprint of Periplus Editions (HK) Ltd.

www.tuttlepublishing.com

Copyright © 2025 by Héctor García

Library of Congress Cataloging-in-Publication Data for this book is in progress

ISBN 978-4-8053-1804-9

Distributed by

North America, Latin America & Europe
Tuttle Publishing
364 Innovation Drive,
North Clarendon
VT 05759-9436, USA
Tel: 1 (802) 773 8930
Fax: 1 (802) 773 6993
info@tuttlepublishing.com
www.tuttlepublishing.com

Japan
Tuttle Publishing
Yaekari Building
3rd Floor, 5-4-12 Osaki
Shinagawa-ku
Tokyo 141-0032
Tel: (81) 3 5437-0171
Fax: (81) 3 5437-0755
sales@tuttle.co.jp
www.tuttle.co.jp

Asia Pacific
Berkeley Books Pte. Ltd.
3 Kallang Sector #04-01
Singapore 349278
Tel: (65) 67412178
Fax: (65) 67412179
inquiries@periplus.com.sg
www.tuttlepublishing.com

28 27 26 25   5 4 3 2 1
Printed in China   2412CM